SHELLEY'S
Prometheus Unbound

SHELLEY'S
Prometheus Unbound

⋲ A CRITICAL READING ⋺

BY EARL R. WASSERMAN

THE JOHNS HOPKINS PRESS BALTIMORE 1965

❧ CONTENTS ❧

SHELLEY'S
Prometheus Unbound

CHAPTER I

◄§ BEING §►

HAMLET's fate, Shelley is reported to have said, was
meant to represent the tragic errors to which the profoundly philosophic mind is liable because it contem-
plates reality as wholly subjective, that is, as a body of
ideas in the mind.[1] Very nearly the first of Hamlet's
words, "Seems, madam! Nay, it is; I know not 'seems,'"
appeared to Shelley a confirmation of Hamlet's solip-
sism. Since reality exists only in Hamlet's mind, what
"seems" to him to be is all that is. "Observe, too," Shelley
continued of Hamlet—

> Observe, too, when Horatio tells him of this wonderful
> appearance [of the ghost], how philosophical his ques-
> tions are, as of a man trying to realise completely, in his
> own mind, the image of the thing. The mysterious contra-
> diction between reality and ideality, one of the most pro-
> found questions of ontology, is strongly shown in the

[1] *New Monthly Magazine and Literary Journal*, n.s. XXIX, pt. ii (1830),
327–36. This dialogue between "Shelley" and "Byron" on the subject
of *Hamlet* purports to have been recorded by a companion of the poets.
An abbreviated version, taken from *The Polar Star*, V (1830), is re-
printed in Walter E. Peck's *Shelley, His Life and Work* (Boston, 1927),
II, 421–32. In "Shelley's Last Poetics: A Reconsideration" (in *From Sensibility to Romanticism*, ed. F. W. Hillis and H. Bloom [New York,
1965], pp. 487–511) I have offered my reasons for believing the dialogue authentic.

beginning of this dialogue. "My father! methinks I see my father!"—"O where, my Lord?" cries Horatio, starting in terror. "In my mind's eye, Horatio." To this subject Hamlet recurs again, in the conversation with his two good friends: "There is," says he, "nothing either good or bad, but thinking makes it so." And again in another place, where Osric asks "if he knows Laertes?" he replies, "I dare not confess that, lest I should compare with him in excellence; for to know a man well were to know oneself."

Then, when the ghost has charged Hamlet with his duty, Hamlet "confuses his external body with his inner self, as if he were nothing but a spirit; and when he says that he will raze out all that he learned from experience or from thought,

> 'And thy commandment all alone shall live
> Within the book and volume of my brain':

he takes out his real tablets and writes it down."

Apart from the interest we may find in this quasi-Coleridgean reading as literary interpretation, it has the value of showing that Shelley held up Shakespeare's play as a mirror in which to look at his own philosophic concerns. His inclination to read *Hamlet* in terms of a special ontology hints at how crucial to him that problem is and how readily he seizes on the possibility of a world constituted of thoughts. For Shelley's Hamlet is Shelley himself, trying vainly to transcend the mortal state, which bewilderingly splits reality into subject and object, thought and thing, being and seeming. His definition of the ghost of Hamlet's father as "an outward and visible sign of the sudden apparitions of the mysterious world within us" and as "a great purpose coming suddenly upon a meditative mind," that is, as a translation of mental modes into sensible qualities, suggests the symbolic externalizing of mental acts and powers in *Prometheus Unbound*—the Furies, the Spirits of the Human Mind, Panthea's dreams, Hercules. And Shelley's interest in the confusion, exchange, and interdependence in Hamlet of ideal and real, subjective and objective—the writing on the tablet, for example—recalls his account of the poetic method of *Prometheus Unbound,* a method he claimed to find pre-eminently in the Greeks and Dante, but also in Shakespeare: "The imagery which I have employed will be found, in many instances, to have been drawn from the operations of the human mind, or from those external actions by which they are expressed." Shelley's bias, all this suggests, is to speculate on the possibility that the "external" is in some fashion a function of the mind. Read against the analysis of *Hamlet,* the similar description of the symbolic method of his own drama intimates that *Prometheus Unbound* takes place in the framework of his own solution of "the most profound questions of ontology" and of his resolution of the "mysterious contradiction between reality and ideality."

Is there a substantive reality independent of the mind? or is the "external" world a function of mind? What is the relation between mind and its perceptions? and is there a sense in which all the thoughts of the mind are real? Is there an externally given standard of good, or does "thinking make it so"? On these questions Shelley meditated earnestly throughout his life, and largely because his poetry usually supposes a special ontology in a more than ordinarily crucial way and because that ontology is remote from most men's habitual assumptions, many of his poems have remained somewhat less than accessible.

[3]

Prior to the time when he composed *On Life*, Shelley, by his own confession in that essay, had rejected both materialism, which denies the existence of anything but matter and motion, and "the shocking absurdities of the popular philosophy of mind and matter," a dualism that he seems still to have entertained in 1812, when he wrote *Queen Mab*, but that he had repudiated by 1816, when he wrote *Mont Blanc*. By that date, if not earlier, partly because he detected in the dualism of matter and spirit the basis of the Christian doctrine of a divine Creator,[2] he appears to have settled upon a body of speculations that he occasionally called the "intellectual philosophy," a term that intimates a monistic ontology based exclusively upon an examination of the data and operations of the mind.[3] Although this doctrine as outlined in the prose fragments Mary Shelley entitled *On Life* and *Speculations on Metaphysics* has obvious affinities with

[2] Its "violent dogmatism concerning the source of all things" (*On Life*).
[3] In the Morgan Library MS of the essay *On Life*, the date of which cannot be settled with any certainty, Shelley wrote of both the "intellectual philosophy" and the "intellectual system," opposed it to the "mind-material philosophy," and described it as the logical inference to be drawn from the idealistically inclined skepticism of Sir William Drummond's *Academical Questions* (London, 1805): "Examined point by point, and word by word, the most discriminating intellects have been able to discern no train of thoughts in the process of its reasoning [i.e., of Drummond's book] which does not conduct inevitably to the conclusion which has been stated [i.e., the "intellectual philosophy"]." (This sentence in the MS, like a number of others, has not hitherto been transcribed accurately.) Among the notes following the essay Shelley also wrote, "No distinction between mind & matter; —the intellectual system—."

In a fictitious dialogue, which could not have been written prior to late 1820, Shelley was still using the term and opposing it to materialism. Referring to someone who had complained of the sophistries of his thought, he wrote, "Such is your conception of the intellectual ⟨philosophy⟩ system of which Lionel [i.e., Shelley] is a disciple. The mechanical philosophy of the day which is popular because it is superficial, and intelligible because it is conversant alone with the grosser objects of our

Berkeley's (and in some aspects with Hume's skepticism), it crucially omits Berkeley's God and is drawn out to conclusions that not only are intolerable to the Berkeleian system but considerably exceed the limits of any reasoned and systematic philosophizing. Indeed, to seek out Shelley's theory of reality in any one philosophic system or in any mere assembly of antecedent doctrines, whatever the partial similarities or even obvious borrowings, can result only in distortion. In particular, our understanding of Shelley has suffered severely from the uncritical assumption that he must be a Platonist, for his indisputable interest in some passages of the Platonic dialogues has led many readers, wholly inferentially, to import and superimpose upon his poetry alien Platonic doctrines, instead of constructing out of Shelley's own statements the pattern of ideas that is peculiarly his own. Shelley's thought must be understood as generically derived from British empiricism and its eighteenth-century developments, which more than ever had made the problems of ontology crucial. The direction his thinking took was determined by his efforts to settle in his own way the kinds of questions raised by the British empiricists, whose heirs the Romantics were, not by his conviction of

⟨sensations⟩ thought. . . ." (I have simplified this heavily revised passage in Bodleian MS Shelley adds. e.8, fol. 71, without, I hope, affecting its sense. For its date, see Neville Rogers, *Shelley at Work* [Oxford, 1956], pp. 17, 257.)

Drummond (p. 135) writes of the "intellectual system, which I consider as founded upon the highest probability," and the context makes it apparent that he means a metaphysics based on the reality of "intellectual *phaenomena*" and opposed to a matter-spirit ontology. The sentence opens a chapter that refutes Cartesian dualism. To Shelley's contemporaries the term "intellectual" apparently suggested any form of philosophical idealism. Hazlitt, for example, described Coleridge's *Biographia Literaria* as "promising us an account of the Intellectual System of the Universe" (*Works,* ed. A. R. Waller and A. Glover, X, 138).

the truth of any one philosopher's system; and his abundant recourse to the ancient philosophers was an eclectic search for partial aid in his quest. Locke's unsatisfactory theory of substance and qualities, Berkeley's God-based idealism, and Hume's skepticism had bequeathed to the early nineteenth century a universe whose location and constitution were disturbingly uncertain; and the Romantic was inevitably challenged to define reality and the mind's relation to it if he was to live in any meaningful way and to settle on the nature and values of experience. "There was a time in my life," Wordsworth once said, "when I had to push against something that resisted, to be sure that there was anything outside me. I was sure of my own mind; everything else fell away, and vanished into thought." [4] This is an honest report of a real psychological experience, but it also epitomizes the ontological consequences that flow out of eighteenth-century empiricism and hence out of the uncertain metaphysics that the Romantics, individually, were required to resolve.

Since Shelley has left us only fragmentary prose meditations, most of which cannot be dated with certainty, and since it is highly unlikely that he ever formulated a wholly coherent and systematic philosophy or consistently adhered to the same rigid philosophic construct, it is necessary to fashion the connective outlines of his thought by placing his explicit declarations in the context of the ontological problem that empiricism had created for him and of the philosophic idealism toward which empiricism compels. In the attempt that follows in this chapter to establish the philosophic setting of *Prometheus Unbound,* the assumption will be that Shelley is not a Platonist or Neoplatonist or skeptic or Berke-

[4] *Poetical Works,* ed. E. de Selincourt and H. Darbishire (Oxford, 1947), IV, 467.

leian (despite Mary Shelley's statement to the contrary), or indeed a disciple of any other philosopher, but that his thought is as much the direct outgrowth of contemporary intellectual forces as Kant's or Coleridge's or Schelling's and that his palpable appropriations from, say, Plato are eclectically determined by the internal requirements of his own brand of evolving idealism. Indeed, in many of its features Shelley's thought closely resembles that of the German post-Kantians, precisely because the historical situation presented them with approximately the same questions in approximately the same philosophic context. Like any other searching mind, Shelley's unquestionably drew upon much of his philosophic reading—Plato, Lucretius, Spinoza, Berkeley, Hume, d'Holbach, Sir William Drummond, Godwin, among many others—not because he ever entered into discipleship with any one philosopher, but because each offered some partial doctrine that, abstracted from its original defining system, could support or advance the special metaphysics he was trying to think through for himself.

II

By the time he was eighteen Shelley had entirely rejected the Christian myth, its ethics based on rewards and punishments, and its ethical sanctions based on a divine moral Governor, and he was puzzling over the effects of this repudiation on his metaphysics. By mid-1811, after a brief struggle, he also relinquished belief in a divine Creator, or First Cause,[5] and accepted what he

[5] See his letters to Hogg, 3 Jan., 12 Jan., and 17 May 1811. (All references to Shelley's letters will be to the edition by Frederick L. Jones

had already written, no doubt under pressure from Hogg, in *The Necessity of Atheism:* "It is easier to suppose that the Universe has existed from all eternity, than to conceive a being capable of creating it." The most compelling force in the development of Shelley's ideas thereafter is the vacuum thus created by his continuous and consistent denial of a transcendent, omnipotent Maker who imposes upon man a code of conduct and punishes or rewards in proportion to the observance of it. With this theistic ground of existence and value removed, Shelley's principles are germinated by his lifelong quest for some other absolute or absolutes. In 1811–1812, energetically devoting himself to the problem, he settled upon a form of pantheism by substituting an immanent intellect for a transcendent anthropomorphic deity: God is the world-soul, the infused mind animating the material universe. Even before abandoning the idea of a Creator, he had defined God as "the Soul of the Universe, the intelligent & *necessarily* [and not, as he conceived of the Christian God, arbitrarily] beneficent actuating principle," some "vast intellect" that "animates Infinity." [6] Thereafter, denying a divine Creator, he was soon teaching Elizabeth Hitchener that God is to the universe

> as the soul of man to his body, as the vegetative power to vegetables, the stony power to stones. . . . In this sense I acknowledge a God, but merely as a synonime for the *existing power of existence*. I do not in *this* . . . recognise a Being which has created that to which it is confessedly annexed as an essence, as that without which

---

[Oxford, 1964].) Shelley's fullest and most explicit denial of a *"creative* Deity,"of course, is his note to *Queen Mab* (1813) on this subject. See also his much later *On the Devil and Devils.*
[6] Letter to Hogg, 3 Jan. 1811.

the universe wd. not be what it is, it is therefore the *essence* of the universe, the universe is the essence of it— it is another *word* for the essence of the universe.[7]

For a number of years Shelley was to cling to this pantheism resulting from the rejection of a transcendent Author of the universe. "Power," he has the self-defeating Christian argue in his *Refutation of Deism* (1814), is the "attribute," or essential quality, of "being," not the "origin" of it; and the words "God" and "universe" must be synonymous because, since the infinite includes the finite, the distinction between "the Universe and that by which the Universe is upheld is manifestly erroneous." God is "a pervading Spirit co-eternal with the universe."[8] Moreover, this world-soul, which is the source of all activity, including life itself, is an intelligence, although not an arbitrary one, a mind within, as Virgil had described it, that pervades, sustains, and sways the whole universe.[9] Causation, animation, and intelligence are all one; and the term "God" designates the "animative intellect" of the whole "mass of organized animation," or the "mass of infinite intelligence" of which "I, you, & he are constituent parts."[10] In brief, at this stage Shelley admitted only an eternal material universe and an infused coexisting spirit that is the essence of being and is, without differentiation, power, life, and mind. Beyond these two there is nothing. This metaphysical model was to be redesigned and modified in crucial ways, but it is the basis from which Shelley's subsequent thought was to evolve.

The major reformation of this doctrine came about mainly through Shelley's gradual rejection of the dual-

[7] Letter to Elizabeth Hitchener, 11 June 1811.
[8] Note to *Queen Mab*.   [9] *Aeneid* vi. 726–27.
[10] Letters to Elizabeth Hitchener, 24 Nov. 1811 and 2 Jan. 1812.

ism of mind and matter on which it was originally founded. In 1812, with remarkable misunderstanding of what he had read, he refused Berkeley's immaterialism; [11] yet, in late 1813 he confessed in bewilderment the logicality of "Hume's reasonings with respect to the non-existence of external things" and admitted that they follow from Locke's empiricism.[12] Although we cannot date the fragments *On Life* and *Speculations on Metaphysics,* they elaborate the philosophic idealism that Shelley then arrived at; and I mean to propose that their doctrines are basic assumptions in *Prometheus Unbound.*

Like Berkeley, Shelley came to hold that it is only by means of a fiction that we separate sensible ideas from the mental act of perception and assign to them a materiality of which we have no experience. Our perceptions obviously can exist only in the mind and can exist there only by virtue of the mind's awareness of them. Not matter, therefore, but awareness is the stuff of which being is made, and the radical form of awareness is self-consciousness, the mind's experience of itself.[13] Conse-

---

[11] Letter to Godwin, 29 July 1812. In his *Essay on Sepulchres* (1809) Godwin had acknowledged that he was "more inclined to the opinion of the immaterialists, than of the materialists" (pp. 5–6).

[12] Letter to Hogg, 26 Nov. 1813.

[13] Shelley's rejection of materialism and the dualism of mind and matter was continuous after about 1813. Occasionally, it is true, he employed the word "matter," but only as a concession to the popular vocabulary. His eagerness to adjust the term to his own immaterialism is suggested by the following characteristic passage in his (no doubt late) essay *On the Devil and Devils.* The Greek dualists "accounted for evil by supposing that what is called matter is eternal" and that it resisted the efforts of God to give it perfect "arrangement." This hypothesis, Shelley explains, Christian theologians rejected "on the ground that the eternity of matter is incompatible with the omnipotence of God." "This hypothesis [i.e., of the Greeks], though rude enough, is in no respect very absurd and contradictory. The refined speculations respecting the existence of external objects by which the idea of matter is suggested; to which Plato has the merit of first having directed the attention of the

quently, "Nought is but that which feels itself to be": [14] being and mind, inasmuch as mind is its awareness of itself, are interchangeable terms.[15] This is by no means the same as his earlier doctrine that the universal Mind is the "existing power of existence" or the "essence" of the universe; it removes all distinction between being and mind. However, Shelley is careful to guard against the possible inference from this that what we call perceptions are but modifications of the mind or that the mind generates its own content: "the mind cannot create, it can only perceive." [16] There must be something perceived, and immaterialism does not mean the nonexistence or only illusory existence of sensible objects. The Lockean doctrine that everything in the mind results from perception Shelley had held long before the development of his "intellectual philosophy," for if mind could create, his consistent denial of a Creator would lose its central premise. Yet, even though the mind does not generate its perceptions, their existence is a function of its awareness, and "nothing exists but as [i.e., inasmuch as and in the manner that] it is perceived," as Shelley never ceased repeating. The mind is intuitively conscious of itself and sensorily aware of those received percepts that we call the "external" world; and these awarenesses, taken together, constitute reality to the in-

thinking part of mankind. . . ." At this point the MS breaks off, but it is clear that Shelley means both to affirm the eternity of the "external" world and to claim that its materiality is a fiction. (This interpretation is based on the text as it appears in Bodleian MS Shelley adds. e.9, not on the published transcriptions.)

[14] *Hellas*, 785.

[15] Compare: "It is infinitely improbable that the cause of *mind, that is, of existence,* is similar to mind" (*On Life;* italics mine).

[16] *On Life.* Letter to Leigh Hunt, 27 Sept. 1819: ". . . a doctrine, of which even then [i.e., in 1812] I had long been persuaded, and on which I have founded much of my persuasions, regarding the imagined cause of the Universe—'Mind cannot create, it can only perceive.' "

dividual mind. Mind is Being, not the cause of it, nor its pervading spirit.

The soft spot in Locke's ontology had of course been his pseudoexplanation of what underlies the primary qualities of objects. To say that they are supported by a material substance which is independent of the qualities it stands under and yet cannot be experienced in itself was recognized by Berkeley as meaningless; [17] and for this material substance Berkeley substituted the divine Mind, which both sustains these ideas, or sensible objects, by perceiving them and imprints them on our minds. It is at this point that Shelley and Berkeley must part irreconcilably, since Shelley denies the existence of a divine Mind independent of, and in any way antecedent to, the human mind, and since his other postulate, "mind cannot create, it can only perceive," asserts that it is not the nature of mind, divine or human, to cause what we call reality. Shelley's essential task, therefore, was to transform his earlier pantheistic dualism into a monistic subjective idealism without being forced thereby to reintroduce, in the manner of Berkeley, a transcendent deity as the ground of being. Now, for Berkeley the universe, because it exists in the divine Mind, would continue to exist even though no human mind were to observe it, and thereby he managed to keep the human mind and the sensory universe distinct. The tree will continue in the divine Mind and hence be present even when no human mind is about in the quad. But because subjective idealism defines the universe in terms of perceptions, its inherent logic tends toward an ultimate fusion of subject and object, being and percep-

---

[17] As Shelley understood: "But matter deprived of qualities is an abstraction, concerning which it is impossible to form an idea" (*Refutation of Deism*).

tion; and Berkeley's God and Kant's two worlds are rather desperate efforts to hypothesize a transcendence that will keep the two apart. Without some such autonomous transcendence, philosophic idealism is inclined to merge mind and universe totally, whether the results be the Absolutes of Fichte, Schelling, Hegel, or F. H. Bradley. In brief, unless a duality of the transcendent and the human is superimposed upon this metaphysics, it tends to formulate the distinction between the One and the Many only as the difference between absolute being and its constituent partial modes. Such an absolute being, or universal mind, is neither a God apart from man nor an abstraction, but the reality in which all apparent parts and distinctions are dissolved.

The "solid universe of external things," Shelley had come to believe, "is 'such stuff as dreams are made of' "; [18] and he meant this literally. Having denied himself both Locke's "substance" and Berkeley's God as the ground of the sensible world, he had no choice but to allow subject and object to merge into an identity, since both have their reality in a common awareness. The distinction between the human mind, or self-awareness, and its sensory perception, or awareness of sensible ideas, has meaning only in the context of our imperfect and illusory mortal state as distinct human minds. It is ultimately false, Shelley held, not because the mind creates its own content, but because the mind and its perceptions are really subsumed, monistically, in an eternal reality to which, after the manner of the Romantics, he assigns the name "Life," meaning by it, as he did earlier, that which is, without distinction, both animation and intellect.[19]

[18] *On Life.*
[19] In his essay *A Future State* Shelley twice writes of "the vital & intellectual principle" (singular: the published transcriptions are in error); writes of "life or thought" as interchangeable terms for the same thing;

When we were children, he writes, we

> less habitually distinguished all that we saw and felt,
> from ourselves. They seemed, as it were, to constitute
> one mass. There are some persons who in this respect are
> always children. Those who are subject to the state called
> reverie [20] feel as if their nature were dissolved into the
> surrounding universe, or as if the surrounding universe
> were absorbed into their being. They are conscious of
> no distinction. And these are states which precede, or
> accompany, or follow an unusually intense and vivid ap-
> prehension of life.[21]

Obviously Shelley would have agreed with the objective
idealism of Schelling, which elaborates the absolute "in-

and writes that "Life and thought differs indeed from every thing else"
(the published transcripts, which record "differ," are again in error) and
that ". . . thought and life is . . ." (Bodleian MS Shelley adds. e.11).
    Starting from a quite different premise—a Platonistic triadic hier-
archy—Thomas Taylor also came to the conclusion that in the soul
animation, intellect, and being are one: *"being in it is life and intellect;
life is intellect and essence; and intellect is essence and life.* For there
is one simplicity in it, and one substance" (*The Works of Plato,* trans.
Thomas Taylor [London, 1804], I, 513).
[20] The Morgan MS of the essay *On Life* shows that Shelley intended to
identify these as "Poets & Persons of a peculiar enthusiasm."
[21] *On Life.* The same theme also appears in two manuscript fragments
apparently intended for *Epipsychidion.* In one, Shelley writes that in
infancy

> every thing familiar seems to be
> Wonderful, and the immortality
> Of the great world, which all things must inherit
> Is felt as one with the awakening spirit
> Unconscious of itself, & of the strange
> Distinctions, which in its proceeding change
> It feels & knows, and mourns as if each were
> A desolation . . .
> (Bodleian MS Shelley adds. c.4, folder 3)

The other passage (C. D. Locock, *Examination of the Shelley Manu-
scripts* [Oxford, 1903], p. 13) reads:

> And we will move possessing & possesst
> Wherever beauty on the earth's bare [?] breast
> Lies like thy shadow of thy soul—till we
> Become one being with the world we see.

The lines of the finished poem into which this last passage developed

difference" of the subject-object distinction and teaches that all philosophy consists in a recollection of the condition in which we were one with nature.[22] Only through continued immersion in mortal existence, Shelley argues, through feelings and reasonings that are the "result of a multitude of entangled thoughts, of a series of what are called impressions, planted by reiteration," are we led into the illusion that there is a real distinction between self-consciousness and the world that exists by virtue of our consciousness of it: "in living we lose the apprehension of life." [23] What truly exists, Shelley wrote in a sentence that could have been written by Coleridge or Schelling, is "Life," which "includes all"; and it is for this reason that his fullest sketch of an ontology is mainly on the subject of life and that it begins, "Life, and the world, or whatever we call that which we are and feel, *is* an astonishing thing" (italics mine). Although the repeated reappearance of the same sensible ideas leads one to assume a duality of his own existence and his perceptions, one most nearly participates in being when, in an act that hovers between sensory perception and introspection, this distinction melts into a pure vitalism, which is the same as pure intelligence. There is no need of a divine Mind distinct from human minds to sustain a universe: in fact, both what we customarily call the "universe" and what we customarily call the "human mind" result from a fractured vision of eternal and self-

---

help clarify how the subsumption of the subject and object into each other constitutes both love and life:

> Possessing and possessed by all that is
> Within that calm circumference of bliss,
> And by each other, till to love and live
> Be one. . . .   (*Epipsychidion,* 549–52)

[22] *Sämmtliche werke* (Stuttgart, 1856), I (4), 77.
[23] *On Life.* Unless otherwise specified, all subsequent quotations in this chapter will be from this essay or *Speculations on Metaphysics.*

supporting "Life." Or if we choose to speak of the "universe" it must be understood as the mass of our knowledge, "including our own nature," by which Shelley means our intuition of ourselves.

Such a conception of being as that radical condition in which the false dichotomy of sensation and self-consciousness vanishes accounts for the strikingly circuitous expression to which Shelley resorted in an effort to describe his "ecstatic wonder, not unallied to madness" upon beholding the oneness and immediacy of the scene at Mont Blanc: "all was as much our own, as if we had been the creators of such impressions in the mind of others as now occupied our own." [24] It would seem as though Shelley were imagining that, as creator of impressions in the minds of others, he were like Berkeley's God; but at any rate it is evident that he is trying to express the absolute, unmediated identity of the human perceiving mind and its perceptions. Moreover, by tracing the illusion of duality to continued mortal existence, Shelley leaves open the possibility not only of a preexistence in which the unity of mind and the perceived universe was unfractured but also of such a postmortal return. Consequently, in *Prometheus Unbound*, although the dead express the possibility that they, like mortals, may "change and pass away," Demogorgon proposes the alternative, that death is the identity of being and perception:

> Whether your nature is that universe
> Which once ye saw and suffered—.[25]

(IV. 536–37)

---

[24] Letter to Peacock, 22–28 July 1816.
[25] The canceled manuscript reading is helpfully suggestive: ". . . fills the Universe / Which living ye beheld & felt . . ." (Huntington MS 2176, fol. 16ᵛ).

And this same reunion of the human soul with the "external" universe is one mode of the immortality of Adonais, who in death is "made one with Nature" and is "a portion of the loveliness / Which once he made more lovely." [26]

Given, however, the mortal illusion of a duality of mind and universe, it is important to assign to the supposedly external its true ontological status. If nothing exists but as it is perceived, the word "thing," Shelley argued, properly designates "any object of thought," and since therefore it is a thought, it must be defined, not with respect to any supposedly external existence, but exclusively as a thought: a "thing" is "any thought upon which any other thought is employed with an apprehension of distinction." It is meaningless, then, to consider the question of whether "thought" is distinct from "the objects of thought," the object of a thought being a thought. Since sensible "objects" exist only by virtue of being perceived and are not created by mind, the terms "external" and "internal" are equally irrelevant, and it is a matter of indifference whether we say "that when speaking of the objects of thought, we indeed only describe one of the forms of thought—or that, speaking of thought, we only apprehend one of the operations of the universal system of beings." Neither alone is absolutely right, for the "forms of thought" and the "universal system of beings" are really identical. Thus in making the customary philosophic distinction between impressions and ideas in terms of vividness and obscurity, Shelley describes the universe both as the "system of beings" ("Now dark—now glittering") and as "forms of thought" ("now reflecting [the mind's] gloom— / Now lending [to the mind] splendour").[27] Each mind is "at once the

[26] *Adonais*, 371, 378–79.　　[27] *Mont Blanc*, 3–4.

[17]

centre and the circumference": the center "to which all things are referred" because that which is outside the self exists by virtue of the mind's awareness of it; and the "line within which all things are contained" because the object of thought is one with the mind's thoughts. But center and circumference in fact coincide, and the dualism of "internal" and "external" is as false as that of self-awareness and awareness of sensible ideas.

By assuming without question the "Author of Nature," Berkeley had a basis for claiming a categorical distinction not only between human minds and the sensible world but also between "real things" and "chimeras." Real things are the ideas imprinted on the senses by the Author of Nature and are regular, vivid, and constant because of God's uniform workings; chimeras are ideas of the mind's own compounding and lack these assuring qualities. But without a Creator Shelley had no ground for claiming that only regular, vivid, and constant ideas are real. The popular distinction between those "two classes of thought" called "ideas" and "external objects" is purely nominal; and while those thoughts called "real" and "external" are indeed characterized by their being clear, distinct, and regular and common in recurrence, they are not otherwise different from thoughts arising in "hallucinations, dreams, and the ideas of madness." The only true criterion of the former class of thoughts is their being the "most invariably subservient to the security and happiness of life" as a mere practical fact, but they are not therefore generically and essentially different. Nor are hallucinations to be considered fictions, for there are no ontological criteria to distinguish fiction from reality: because "we can think of nothing which we have not perceived" and because all knowledge is "bounded by perception, whose operations may be indefinitely combined," hallucinations are only "modes in which thoughts are combined" and therefore, Shelley adds, must be included in the "catalogue of existence." Everything that is thought exists because it is thought. Thus the true science would be a classification, not of "things" as distinct from "thoughts" nor of the "real" as distinct from the "chimerical," but of all thoughts "graduated according to the degrees of a combined ratio of intensity, duration, connection, periods of recurrence, and utility." All these thoughts, "including our own nature," constitute "what we call the universe." It is for this reason that Asia can say that all the "living world" contains is the content of the mind: "thought, passion, reason, will, / Imagination" (II. iv. 10–11). And, correspondingly, in *Hellas* Ahasuerus adds that only thought and its living ("quick") elements, Will, Passion, Reason, and Imagination, are immortal; woven by mutability into unstable and transient configurations, they constitute what we illusorily experience as the mutable "external" world (795–801). Man erroneously assumes an external world on which mutability acts, whereas the "external" is but the perceptions of the mental faculties. Projected into what seems to be an independent outwardness and cast into mutable arrangements, the contents of the mind's faculties are called the universe. But in fact it is the immutable faculties, not their "external" thoughts, that are woven by mutability into what is believed to be the mutable world: "They are, what they regard appears" (798). It is strikingly in harmony with his subjective idealism, incidentally, that in these words Shelley identifies the seemingly "external" in terms of an act of perception ("regard").

That the idealism we have been describing up to this

[19]

point is indeed to be understood as the metaphysical setting of *Prometheus Unbound* is made fairly evident by
Asia's description of one of Prometheus' gifts:

> He gave man speech, and speech created thought,
> Which is the measure of the universe.
>
> (II. iv. 72–73)

Shelley's theory of language must be considered later,
but it is clear that by "created" he meant "shaped" or
"ordered" into palpable forms, since we are later told
that language "rules . . . a throng / Of thoughts and
forms, which else senseless and shapeless were" (IV.
416–17). What is significant at the moment is the statement that thought is "the measure of the universe." Protagoras' aphorism, of which this clearly is an adaptation,
teaches that "Man is the measure of all things"; and from
his reading of Diogenes Laertius and Plato, among
others, Shelley would have understood this to mean that
man is the measure "of the existence of the things that
are and of the non-existence of things that are not" and
that "of the real things, . . . their reality is a separate
one for each person." [28] Being is relative to the mind's
perceptions; or, in Asia's terms, the universe is proportional to thought. The same ontological idealism reappears as the theme of Prometheus' definition of works of
art. They are

> lovely apparitions, dim at first,
> Then radiant, as the mind, arising bright
> From the embrace of beauty, whence the forms
> Of which these are the phantoms, casts on them
> The gathered rays which are reality.
>
> (III. iii. 49–53)

[28] Diogenes Laertius *Lives of Eminent Philosophers* ix. 51; Plato *Theaete-
tus* 152a. In Cicero's *Academia* (ii. 142) Shelley would have read, "Aliud
iudicium Protagorae est qui putet id cuique verum esse quod cuique

From some absolute beauty the mind's shapeless apparitions derive their forms. But whereas man normally supposes that the phantoms of darkness reveal themselves as self-sustaining realities when the rising sun illuminates and defines them clearly, in fact it is the rays of the mind that, being cast on them, constitute their reality.

Now, given such an inclusive definition of "reality," or the "universe," it follows that the distinctions among physics, metaphysics, and moral philosophy, like the difference between thing and thought, must become merely nominal, indicating not differences in kinds of subject matter, but only differences in the perspectives in which thoughts are viewed. If the universe is thought, passion, reason, will, and imagination, then metaphysics is "the science of all that we know, feel, remember, and believe inasmuch as our knowledge, sensations, memory, and faith constitute the universe considered relatively to human identity"; it is the exact classification of the mind's ideas. Similarly, moral science is "the determination of the arrangement of [all the mind's ideas] which produces the greatest and most solid happiness." Therefore, although metaphysics and ethics apply the same materials to different ends, it is "presumptuous" to assume a real "distinction between the moral and material universe."

Like Berkeley, Shelley also denies the reality of time, space, and motion. Since nothing exists but as it is perceived and since we do not perceive pure time, space, or motion, these supposed entities, Shelley held, must be nothing more than the continually changing relations of our perceptions with respect to the perceiving mind or to

videatur" ("One view of the criterion [of reality] is that of Protagoras, who holds that what seems true to each person is true for each person"). See also Aristotle *Metaphysics* iii. 5.

each other; they are only schemata abstracted from the forms in which our disparate sensations are arranged. It would then seem to follow that if man could release himself from the illusion that separates his being from his perceiving, these relationships would also disappear, and the fictions of time, space, and motion would vanish in the immutable, infinite, and eternal. "What has thought / To do with time, or place, or circumstance?" [29]

Shelley was well aware of the trap toward which his philosophy was leading him. Thing and thought, external and internal, are one; time and space are unreal; and self-consciousness and perception are subsumed under an eternal and self-sustaining "Life." Such is the constitution of what truly is, behind the veil of illusions. But Shelley recognized that the very existence, however illusory, of the individual human mind is contingent upon its experience of separateness and diversity; and the frustrating dilemma that forever racks Shelley is the desire, on the one side, to attain and express the undifferentiated oneness of reality and, on the other, the fact that the only human means to that end are the diversities in which mortal man is bound. Those diversities of relationships among percepts and self that we call time and space, Shelley wrote, are "essential, considered relatively to human identity, for the existence of the human mind." Although "Life" is the undifferentiated union of our "nature" (or self-awareness) and those thoughts that we call the universe, such a oneness, although it is the reality we aspire to, is destructive of the conditions essential to human existence, which depends upon the illusion of diversity and the separateness of the self from its perceptions. For, Shelley added, "if the inequalities, produced by what has been termed the operations of the external

[29] *Hellas*, 801-2.

universe [but are actually the changing modes of the existence of 'things' relative to each other and the perceiving mind] were levelled by the perception of our being [or our 'nature,' or self-awareness] uniting, and filling up their interstices, [which are responsible for our notions of] motion and mensuration, and time, and space; the elements of the human mind being thus abstracted, sensation and imagination cease." "Mind cannot be considered pure" because "impurity" is the necessary condition for the existence of the human mind and of individual human identity. "Silence and solitude," those interstices between sensible ideas, are, Shelley wrote in *Mont Blanc*, a "vacancy," a hiatus creating that illusion of the discreteness and diversity of thoughts on which the individual mind subsists; and yet the purpose of that poem is to reveal, by means of an extraordinary apprehension of the imagination, that behind the illusory there are no such vacancies. In childhood, when we did not habitually distinguish all that we saw and felt from our own being, and when the perceptions of our own being did fill the interstices between "external" perceptions, we most nearly had an apprehension of timeless, spaceless, undifferentiated being and consequently were closest to reality. But we were also, for that very reason, children, individual human minds in only the smallest degree; and any subsequent experience of this identity, like Shelley's in the Vale of Chamounix, is "not unallied to madness," being beyond what is normally human.

Moreover, the "principle of the agreement and similarity of all thoughts, is, that they are thoughts; the principle of their disagreement consists in the variety and irregularity of the occasions on which they arise in the mind." And, Shelley adds, the fact that they are all thoughts is to the variety and irregularity of their occur-

[23]

rences "as everything to nothing." Consequently, even in the individual human mind, which subsists because of the diversities among thoughts, what is essential is the unity of all its thoughts, not their discreteness or differences. It follows for Shelley that the individual mind is a mirror not only *upon* which all separate forms are reflected as thoughts but *in* which "they compose one form." [30] Any one mind is an organized thought.

In sum: what we call the external world exists as an assemblage of thoughts; all the thoughts in the individual mind compose one form; and, united in infinite and eternal "Life," the individual mind's being is identical with its perceptions. But in fact Shelley does not accept even the real existence of a plurality of unitary minds. In the absence of any real distinction between ideas and "external objects" Shelley believed he also had the grounds for the conclusion that "the existence of distinct individual minds . . . is likewise found to be a delusion." Just as the various colors are partial modes of light, so each human mind is but a partial mode of the One Mind, which is the one reality: "The words *I, you, they* are not signs of any actual difference subsisting between the assemblage of thoughts thus indicated, but are merely marks employed to denote the different modifications of the one mind. . . . I am but a portion of it." This "one mind" is obviously not to be understood either as an abstraction or as a deity, but as a metaphysical reality. At least since his rejection of the doctrine of a Creator of the universe, Shelley had been inclined toward a belief that all individual minds are subsumed in a universal mind, and his natural impulse at all times seems to have been to dissolve individual identity in an

[30] Preface to *Prometheus Unbound*.

all-encompassing unity. When in 1812 he formulated a pantheistic dualism requiring an infused animating mind, he concluded that each human mind—"I, you, & he"—is a constituent part of the sustaining "mass of infinite intelligence"; [31] and in *The Daemon of the World* he proposed that every human birth is really the awakening of a portion of the universal mind to sensory experience of the material world that it moves and animates:

> For birth but wakes the universal mind
> Whose mighty streams might else in silence flow
> Thro' the vast world, to individual sense
> Of outward shows, whose unexperienced shape
> New modes of passion to its frame may lend;
> Life is its state of action, and the store
> Of all events is aggregated there
> That variegate the eternal universe.[32]   (539–46)

Now, in the context of a monistic idealism that identifies the One Mind with being instead of making it the animating essence of being, he similarly holds that "The words *I*, and *you*, and *they* are grammatical devices invented simply for arrangement, and totally devoid of the intense and exclusive sense usually attached to them."

[31] Letter to Elizabeth Hitchener, 2 Jan. 1812.
[32] Compare Drummond, *Academical Questions*, pp. 26–27: ". . . the Platonic doctrine, which taught the pre-existence of the immaterial soul, and according to which it was supposed, that the spiritual and incarnate effluence of universal mind, gradually awakes to reminiscence and intelligence, after its first slumber has passed in its corporeal prison." The passage in *Queen Mab* (IX. 155–60), of which the lines quoted from *The Daemon of the World* (pub. 1816) are a revision, differs mainly in using the word "spirit" instead of "universal mind."
It is significant that when Shelley later substituted the "intellectual philosophy" for the pantheistic dualism of *The Daemon of the World* the metaphor likening the universal mind to a river flowing through the world gets reversed: "The everlasting universe of things / Flows through the mind" (*Mont Blanc*, 1–2).

The universal Mind is the same as being, according to the intellectual philosophy, and all human minds are diffused in it.

Earthly life, while a fact in itself, is necessarily a state of illusions, the shadow of the dream in which "nothing is, but all things seem." [33] The mortal condition requires, and is made possible by, the illusion of time, space, and the existence of distinct thoughts and distinct minds; and these illusions and diversities are the sole and necessarily inadequate materials available to earthly man for apprehending and expressing the true unity of being, the only devices he has to lift the veil that conceals truth. What, then, is the relation of the illusory individual minds to the real One Mind? Obviously it is not the relation of human minds to Berkeley's God, who, together with His "ideas," would exist were there no human minds. Nor are we even to assume some Plotinian doctrine of emanations from the One Mind that lead their own earthly existence apart from the One and then return to it. "I am but a portion" of the One Mind, Shelley wrote; and the sense is that human minds and the One Mind do not have separate existences. The One Mind is the metaphysical reality in which all possible human minds are united, in a condition free of the illusions of dualism, diversity, identity, time, and space by virtue of the unity. "The view of life presented by the most refined deductions of the intellectual philosophy," Shelley wrote in the essay *On Life,* "is that of unity"; and we have perhaps failed to recognize how real and unrelenting that doctrine of unity is in Shelley's thought.

However, while the concept of the One Mind provides for the unity of being, it in no way accounts for either

[33] *The Sensitive Plant,* iii. 124.

power or value. We have observed that in his earlier pantheistic days Shelley had postulated a God who is "the intelligent and *necessarily* beneficent, actuating principle" and therefore a sustaining God who is not only mind but also the source of events and the absolute of goodness. When he transformed this pantheistic dualism into an idealistic monism, the sustaining mind became, instead, all of being by subsuming both subject and object, and in that sense it is "Life." But it could no longer be also considered the "actuating principle." In part, Shelley's reason for separating cause from mind is that to assign it to mind is to leave the door open once again to an anthropomorphic governing deity. But more important is his acceptance of Hume's denial that cause is an experiential reality. Shelley never tired of repeating that "when we use the words *principle, power, cause,* &c., we mean to express no real being, but only to class under those terms a certain series of co-existing phenomena," [34] or, again,

> What cause is, no philosopher has succeeded in explaining, and the triumph of the acutest metaphysicians has been confined to demonstrating it to be inexplicable. All we know of cause is that one event, or to speak more correctly, one sensation follows another attended with a conviction derived from experience that these sensations will hereafter be similarly connected. This habitual conviction is that to which we appeal when we say that one thing is the cause of another, or has the power of producing certain effects.[35]

Moreover, as Shelley pointed out in *Mont Blanc,* even though we may trace a series of events back to its first palpable step, that too must be preceded by some prior step because it is not self-generative. This is not to deny

[34] *A Future State.*   [35] *On Polytheism.*

that there is some agency behind every series of sensations and that to this agency the name "power," or
"cause," may properly be given, but since it cannot be
experienced by mind and since, as the ultimate actuating
cause, it acts prior to any palpable event, it cannot be a
part of being as Shelley has defined that word. Mind,
Shelley admitted, "is said also to be the cause" of all
things; and the context makes clear that by "cause" he
means the actuating, not the creative, power.[36] But, he
adds, "cause is only a word expressing a certain state of
the human mind with regard to the manner in which two
thoughts are apprehended to be related to each
other. . . . It is infinitely improbable that the cause of
mind, that is, of existence, is similar to mind." Moreover,
a footnote to *A Refutation of Deism* directs us to Sir William Drummond's declaration that "Power cannot be at
once the principle and the attribute of being." [37] As long
as Shelley had accepted a pantheistic dualism, it was
possible for him to assign power to the immanent unknowable mind that sustains knowable matter, and thus
to dispense with the abhorrent idea of a transcendent actuating deity. Now, however, with the acceptance of the
identity of mind and being, it becomes obligatory to divorce power absolutely from mind-being and yet still to
avoid manufacturing a special divine Mind outside being
to which to assign it. That is, although compelled by his
ontological monism to exclude the mysterious actuating
power from mind-being, Shelley must also be careful to

[36] *On Life.* In the immediately preceding sentences Shelley denies that
mind creates. Rather inexactly using the word "basis" to mean creative
cause, he writes, "that the basis of all things cannot be, as the popular
philosophy [of mind and matter] alleges, mind, is sufficiently evident.
Mind, as far as we have any experience of its properties, and beyond
that experience how vain is argument! cannot create, it can only perceive. It is said also to be the cause. . . ."
[37] *Academical Questions,* p. 5.

prevent the metaphysical principle of cause from becoming a theological reality. His idealistic metaphysics, therefore, provides for a mind-life which is synonymous with being, and, infinitely remote from it, an ultimate, unknowable cause, or power, which is the actuating source and is absolutely different from mind: ". . . the mysterious principle which regulates the proceedings of the universe is neither intelligent nor sensitive. . . ." [38] Consequently he can say of Necessity, or the process by which the ultimate power acts through being,

> No love, no hate thou cherishest; revenge
> And favouritism, and worst desire of fame
> Thou know'st not: all that the wide world contains
> Are but thy passive instruments, and thou
> Regard'st them all with an impartial eye,
> Whose joy and pain thy nature cannot feel,
> Because thou hast not human sense,
> Because thou art not human mind.[39]

When man endows this actuating principle with the characteristics of being—that is, with mind and life—he fabricates the customary superstitious theologies:

> What is that Power? Ye mock yourselves, and give
> A human heart to what ye cannot know:
> As if the cause of life could think and live!
> 'Twere as if man's own works should feel, and show
> The hopes, and fears, and thoughts from which they flow,
> And he be like to them! [40]

Nor, according to the "intellectual philosophy," are the True, the Good, and the Beautiful either identical with the One Mind or attributes of it. Just as Shelley dissociated cause from mind-being, so he also divorced

[38] *A Future State.*   [39] *Queen Mab,* VI. 212–19.
[40] *Revolt of Islam,* VIII. v.

from both a dynamic unitary perfection that is a "Power which models, as they pass, all the elements of this mixed universe to the purest and most perfect shape which it belongs to their nature to assume." [41] Shelley never made clear the relation between the extra-mental power which actuates all events in the realm of being and the extra-mental power which compels being to its own perfection; and it is not evident that he ever considered the question. Nor did he really make clear the relation between being and the compulsion to perfection that lies outside it, except to imply that the One Mind cannot be the same as this force; and yet he seems to have felt that these two together constitute the ultimate perfection of being. The dead Adonais not only is "made one with Nature" and is now "a portion of the loveliness / Which once he made more lovely," subject and object now being one; he is also a "presence"

> Spreading itself where'er that Power may move
> Which has withdrawn his being to its own

and bears

> His part, while the one Spirit's plastic stress
> Sweeps through the dull dense world, compelling there,
> All new successions to the forms they wear;
> Torturing th' unwilling dross that checks its flight
> To its own likeness, as each mass may bear.[42]

Broadly, then, Shelley's intellectual philosophy provides for three distinct absolutes, the One Mind, the one actuating cause, and the one shaping force; and these account, respectively, for being, history, and perfection —reality, agency, and value. Never did he bring these three absolutes together in any systematic metaphysical

[41] *Essay on Christianity.*   [42] *Adonais,* 370–87.

treatise that we know of, nor are all three directly operative factors in the text of any one of his poems. Rather, they are the key members of Shelley's repertory company. Depending upon the thematic objective of a specific poem, one or another of these will take the center of the stage, and the others will be absent or implicit, or will serve subordinate roles.

The essential subject of *Prometheus Unbound* is the One Mind; the extra-mental actuating power is the source of its events; and the drama is the history of the One Mind's evolution into perfection.

III

Any interpretation of *Prometheus Unbound* will necessarily be conditioned by a determination of the drama's area of reference, the level of reality at which it is enacted; and this in turn must be a function of whatever it is that its protagonist represents. Certainly Prometheus is not Man, if we mean by that term the human race. Prometheus himself, avowedly the benefactor and savior of man (I. 817), specifically makes the distinction in an address to Asia:

> we will sit and talk of time and change,
> As the world ebbs and flows, ourselves unchanged.
> What can hide man from mutability?
>
> (III. iii. 23–25)

Unlike man and the world, Prometheus is, at least at this point, immortal and immutable; and Shelley's insistence that only thought, or mind, is eternal demands that we assign Prometheus his role, not in a system of allegorical abstractions, but in a metaphysics of idealism. He must be whatever Shelley's philosophy provides for as eternal and immutable. Moreover, in Act I consolation is brought to him by Spirits who come from the Human Mind, attributes or powers of a state of being necessarily distinct from Prometheus; and therefore he cannot be the Human Mind. Later he prophesies that he and Asia will be visited by the arts of the "human world," which are "mediators / Of that best worship love, by [man] and us / Given and returned" (III. iii. 58–60). Even the speech of Jupiter which is sometimes offered as evidence that Prometheus is the "soul of man" actually distinguishes him from it:

Rejoice! henceforth I am omnipotent.
All else had been subdued to me; alone
The soul of man, like an unextinguished fire,
Yet burns towards heaven with fierce reproach, and doubt,
And lamentation, and reluctant prayer,
Hurling up insurrection. . . .   (III. i. 3–8)

But this cannot apply to Prometheus, who has already retracted his curse; who now pities, not reproaches, and therefore seems to Jupiter to have been subdued; and who never doubted Jupiter's falseness or offered him prayers, however reluctant. Jupiter's words describe his own relation to the "soul of man" in terms of the relation of a god of a theology to his fearful but rebellious human worshipers, and this is precisely the relation into which Prometheus has forever refused to enter. Finally, although the freeing of Prometheus and his reunion with Asia are paralleled by the gradual, progressive improvement of man, there is, explicitly, a significant time lag between the two, as though the continuous process of man's perfecting is in delayed sympathy with the instantaneous event of Prometheus' restoration, or as though one occurred in time and the other outside it.

To assume, then, that Prometheus illustrates "that

man as a soul is not only indestructible, but, through high will inspired by love, is creative," as J. A. Symonds mused; to fancy with Rossetti that he is "that faculty whereby man is man, not brute"; to call him, as Mary Shelley did, "the emblem of the human race" or "the prophetic soul of humanity" or "the mind of mankind" or the "potential state" of man "in so far as it is good," as other critics have speculated; even to lean on Shelley's description of Prometheus as "the type of the highest perfection of moral and intellectual nature, impelled by the purest and the truest motives to the best and noblest ends" [43]—each of these falls short of the mark in so far as it assumes that the central subject of the drama is a mankind having autonomous reality and that Prometheus is an imaginative abstraction of earthly man or his faculties or his ideals. All such interpretations allow for only one mode of existence and neglect the possibility that Shelley's metaphysics provides for two: human minds and the One Mind. Or, rather, they postulate that Prometheus must be a fabricated abstraction drawn by the poet from a reality called "man," instead of postulating the conclusion Shelley's "intellectual system" arrives at—that what we call "real" men are time-bound portions of the One Mind and, with respect to that ultimate reality, are illusory. Individual human minds are indeed a necessary part of the play, but all their actions take place off stage and are effected by sympathy with the Promethean drama; for the human revolution and the history of human perfection that were the subject of the *Revolt of Islam* have here been transposed to the level of ultimate and total being, the metaphysical reality here

[43] In fact, Shelley is not attempting to define his own Prometheus, but is describing the potentiality inherent in the Prometheus of classical myth, or, as he has just said of Satan, the way in which the traditional character "is susceptible of being described."

called "Prometheus." Indeed, except for Demogorgon, Prometheus is the only metaphysical reality actually present in the play, and it would be short of the truth even to say that the drama takes place in his mind; he is the One Mind.

According to the doctrine of Necessity that Shelley embraced, the distinction between good and evil has only human relevance. Rejecting any Manichaean dualism, this doctrine asserts that the infinite power that lies outside being and initiates the processes of the mind and of the universe is neither good nor bad and that Necessity, or the principles whereby those processes take place, is fixed. Not being mind and therefore not having will, the power has no possibility of choice, but asserts itself only as it must. In *Mont Blanc* the snow that falls on the peak of the mountain becomes the murderous glaciers and then the life-giving river; and the one is "evil" and the other "good," not in themselves—for one is the source of the other, and both derive from the ever-falling snow—but only in man's relation to them. Beyond this relative sense of the term, good is the condition resulting from the submission of the mind to the indifferent processes of Necessity, and evil—or, rather, negation of good —must be any willful imposition on the human mind that diverts it from this submission. All such willful impositions Shelley calls "tyranny," the chief agents of which are kings and priests because both claim the existence of an independent authority outside man's mind which dictates arbitrary systems of thought and action and hence prevents submission to Necessity. These arbitrary and tyrannical codes, however, are not real in the sense that the uniform processive patterns of Necessity are real, but are fabricated by the human mind, which then abdicates to these fictions its own powers and enslaves itself to its own creation:

> He who taught man to vanquish whatsoever
> Can be between the cradle and the grave
> Crowned him the King of Life. Oh, vain endeavour!
> If on his own high will, a willing slave,
> He has enthroned the oppression and the oppressor.[44]

It is, therefore, "our will / That thus enchains us to permitted ill." [45] At the heart of this ethical doctrine is the paradox of freedom, which Shelley understands to mean not arbitrary and capricious choice, as though "the will has the power of refusing to be determined by the strongest motive," [46] but only freedom from tyranny, that is, from the artificial, mind-forged restraints that the mind allows itself to impose on itself. Man abandons his natural freedom when he "fabricates / The sword which stabs his peace" and "raiseth up / The tyrant whose delight is in his woe." [47] But true freedom, paradoxically, does not mean freedom from the fixed processes of Necessity, to which the mind must submit itself if it is to possess its own will; for this submission is "that sweet bondage which is Freedom's self," a "weakness" or "meekness" which is strength.[48]

In accordance with these definitions, Shelley has represented in Jupiter all tyrannical evils and has identified him with the conventional God of the theists. But since "evil" is only an efficient fiction constituted of the mind's abdicated powers, Jupiter has no real and independent existence in the sense that either mind or power does. As Mary Shelley reported, "Shelley believed that mankind

[44] *Ode to Liberty*, 241–45.   [45] *Julian and Maddalo*, 170–71.
[46] Note to *Queen Mab*.   [47] *Queen Mab*, III. 199–202.
[48] *Ibid.*, IX. 76; *Prometheus Unbound*, II. iii. 93–94.

[35]

had only to will that there should be no evil, and there would be none," not because it can so easily be wished away, but because it is not an attribute of being—that is, because "evil is not inherent in the system of creation, but an accident that might be expelled." Evil is a lapse of the mind, its negative mode, its reflection in a distorting mirror, and no more independent of Prometheus than that. "What then is God?" Shelley had asked:

> Some moon-struck sophist stood
> Watching the shade from his own soul upthrown
> Fill Heaven and darken Earth, and in such mood
> The Form he saw and worshipped was his own,
> His likeness in the world's vast mirror shown.[49]

Consequently, although Jupiter appears in the drama as a god, he is not a being or an autonomous power, but only a dark shadow of Prometheus himself, an unnatural condition of mind that mind wrongfully permits and can repeal by an act of will. "I gave all / He has," says Prometheus (I. 381–82), because Jupiter is only what he has resigned; and any institutionalizing and reifying of these abdicated mental powers is, by definition, evil, which then demands fearful submission of the mind to its own fiction. Unlike the traditional Jupiter, who usurped the throne of the gods and was merely aided to this end by Prometheus, Shelley's Jupiter is actually enthroned by Prometheus, who gave him "wisdom, which is strength" and "Clothed him with the dominion of wide Heaven" (II. iv. 44, 46). Hence Prometheus can say to Jupiter, "O'er all things but thyself I gave thee power, / And my own will" (I. 273–74). Not only is Jupiter unable to determine the will of Prometheus, the One Mind;

---

[49] *Revolt of Islam*, VIII. vi; and see version in *Laon and Cythna*. Compare also *Revolt of Islam*, X. xxx.

[36]

he is not even self-determining because he exists only through Prometheus' concession that he be, or, rather, because he is only an unnatural phantom surrogate for Prometheus. It is for this reason that the overcoming of Jupiter leaves not a shattered form, but a blank, a "void annihilation": "How art thou sunk, withdrawn, covered, drunk up / By thirsty nothing" (IV. 350–51); and Prometheus knows that when Jupiter's soul is cloven it will "Gape like a hell within" (I. 56). Because evil is not inherent in the system of creation, Mind has "only" to will that there be no evil, and there is none.

When Prometheus decides that his own evil curse against Jupiter not be repeated by "aught resembling me" (I. 220), it is more than a fine irony on his part that he assigns the task of repeating it to the Phantasm of Jupiter; for the audience is thus presented with the dramatic shock of observing the Phantasm of Jupiter in effect mindlessly cursing himself. The curse Prometheus had once spoken is admittedly an evil (I. 219), and if it is proper that it now be repeated by the shadow of him who is all evil, the implication is that when Prometheus first spoke it he was, in a very real sense, Jupiter. Milton Wilson has called attention to the striking similarities between Prometheus' description of the Phantasm about to repeat the curse and Prometheus' self-description contained in the curse itself.[50] In Jupiter's Phantasm Prometheus sees

> the curse on gestures proud and cold,
> And looks of firm defiance, and calm hate,
> And such despair as mocks itself with smiles;
>
> (I. 258–60)

and at once the Phantasm repeats Prometheus' original execration:

[50] *Shelley's Later Poetry* (New York, 1959), pp. 63–64.

Fiend, I defy thee! with a calm, fixed mind,
   All that thou canst inflict I bid thee do;
Foul Tyrant both of Gods and Human-kind.
                                        (I. 262–64)

Indeed, it is impossible to know whether Jupiter's Phantasm reflects the appearance of Jupiter or has dramatically assumed the appearance of Prometheus when he first spoke the curse. But I would suggest it is necessary to go beyond Mr. Wilson's conclusions and understand this as the actual identification of the execrating Prometheus with Jupiter, who is the anthropomorphic God made in the image of Prometheus. Not only does the audience watch the Phantasm of Jupiter uttering the curse against him of whom it is the phantasm; it also observes Prometheus facing his own former self in Jupiter's ghost, since all of Jupiter's nature—pride, coldness, defiance, calm hatred, self-mocking despair—existed in Prometheus when he cursed his oppressor, although he has dispelled these evils from himself now that he no longer hates, but pities. "I am changed so that aught evil wish / Is dead within; . . . no memory [remains] / Of what is hate" (I. 70–72).[51] If Prometheus intends a bitter irony by causing the Phantasm of Jupiter to utter the curse against Jupiter, there is also an irony he does not intend in his believing he has not called up "aught resembling me."

Throughout the play, as we shall see, Jupiter is presented as only a cruel parody of Prometheus, and this relationship is repeatedly underscored in Act I by treating

---

[51] When Prometheus has heard the curse he once uttered, he repents, adding, "I wish no living thing to suffer pain" (I. 305). The reference is mainly to Jupiter, it is obvious, since the curse was directed against him; but it is probably significant that at this point Shelley originally wrote the following stage direction: "he [i.e., Prometheus] bends his head as in pain."

him as the distorted, mocking reflection of Prometheus. Although Panthea sees Prometheus as "firm, not proud" (I. 337), Jupiter's Phantasm, who himself shows "gestures proud," calls him "proud sufferer" (I. 245); and Prometheus, speaking "with a calm, fixed mind," addresses Jupiter as "awful image of calm power" (I. 296), while the Phantasm looks cruel, "but calm and strong, / Like one who does, not suffers wrong" (I. 238–39). In one sense it is Jupiter who fills the world with his "malignant spirit" (I. 276), but in fact it is Prometheus who, in hate, has imprecated on "me and mine . . . / The utmost torture of thy hate" (I. 278–79). Prometheus' struggle is really a contest with himself, and his reference to Jupiter's "self-torturing solitude" (I. 295) is, with the deepest irony, actually a description of his own state as, chained to the precipice, he endures "torture and solitude, / Scorn and despair" (I. 14–15).

If it is sound to define Jupiter as the privative mode of Prometheus, we can understand why Prometheus, addressing Jupiter, describes the universe as

> those bright and rolling worlds
> Which Thou and I alone of living things
> Behold with sleepless eyes! (I. 2–4)

For if the universe is the mass of thought, then it has a continuous existence by virtue of its being the unending perception by the One Mind—and by its negative mode that it has permitted.[52] These alone, like Berkeley's God and unlike the human mind, never cease to perceive the thought that is the universe. But as the institutional reifi-

---

[52] This interpretation is not, of course, obviated by the fact that Prometheus' sleepless vision derives from *Prometheus Bound* 32, and Jupiter's, from the maxim that tyrants dare not sleep (in his manuscript Shelley first wrote of Jupiter, "for a tyrant seldom sleeps, / Thou never") and probably from Pope's translation of *Iliad* ii. 2 ("the ever-wakeful eyes of Jove").

cation of Prometheus' relinquished powers Jupiter would have the One Mind bow in total submission and abandon itself entirely to the then self-determined institution. Therefore, were it not for Prometheus' "all-enduring will" to resist, the One Mind would be deprived of itself, given up entirely to its own negation; and the world that exists because it is perceived would have "vanished, like thin mist / Unrolled on the morning wind" [53] (I. 116–17). Mindlessness can have no thoughts, and thoughtlessness can be the "measure" only of a vacancy.

In his drama Shelley achieves an obvious and powerful expressionistic effect by adapting the natural scene to the stages of Prometheus' unbinding. The slow emergence of day out of night in the wintry Caucasus, for example, is the fitting scenic expression of Prometheus' retraction of his curse; and it is appropriate, for the same reason, that the events initiating the new Promethean order begin in Act II with the first day of spring. But what we have observed of the relation between mind and universe suggests that these settings are more than mere metaphors or stage backgrounds. For if nothing exists but as it is perceived and if thought is the measure of the universe, the state of the "external" world is relative to the condition of the mind. The catalogue of existence is made up not only of the thoughts formed by sensory experience but also of all the "modes in which thoughts are combined," so that a "catalogue of all the thoughts of the mind and of all their possible modifications is a cyclopaedic history of the Universe." [54] If we accept that Prometheus is the One Mind, on which the existence of the universe depends, it is implicit that its mode of exist-

[53] Again, the fact, but not its significance, derives from the plan of Aeschylus' Zeus to destroy the human race and replace it with another (*Prometheus Bound* 233–40).
[54] *Speculations on Metaphysics.*

ence determines the manner in which it modifies those thoughts called "external" and that its being "bound" should necessarily involve a distortion of the world. It is presumptuous, Shelley held, to believe that there is any essential "distinction between the moral and material universe."

In his early reading of the works of the French mechanists, such as Cabanis' *Rapports du physique et du moral de l'homme* and La Mettrie's *L'Homme machine,* Shelley had been impressed by the idea of a simultaneous melioration in the physical and moral worlds, and in his zeal to find grounds for his faith in progress he assumed, as we have seen, a beneficent force driving toward perfection in man and nature alike. "The language spoken . . . by the mythology of nearly all religions," he wrote in 1813, "seems to prove that at some distant period man forsook the path of nature and sacrificed the purity and happiness of his being to unnatural appetites. The date of this event seems to have been that of some great change in the climates of the earth, with which it has an obvious correspondence." [55] Since nature would reassume perfection by returning to the Golden Age of eternal spring, Shelley wished to believe the astronomical tradition according to which the obliquity of the earth's ecliptic, or the inclination of its axis, which is responsible for the varying seasons and the unequal lengths of day and night, is gradually disappearing.[56] "It is exceedingly probable," he felt while he still believed in the dualism of mind and matter,

[55] *A Vindication of Natural Diet;* and note to *Queen Mab.*
[56] Letter to Thomas Hookham [early 1813] (*Letters,* ed. Jones, I, 349): "You would very much oblige me if you would collect all possible documents on the Precession of the Equinoxes; as also anything that may throw light upon the question whether or no the position of the Earth on its poles is not yearly becoming less oblique?"

that this obliquity will gradually diminish, until the equator coincides with the ecliptic: the nights and days will then become equal on the earth throughout the year, and probably the seasons also. There is no great extravagance in presuming that the progress of the perpendicularity of the poles may be as rapid as the progress of the intellect; or that there should be a perfect identity between the moral and physical improvement of the human species.[57]

Although he was soon to learn from his reading of Laplace that science had demonstrated the continuous oscillation of the earth's axis instead of its gradual return to the perpendicular,[58] apparently he was able to sustain his earlier faith on the basis of his subsequent idealism, since it denies any true distinction between mind and world. Just as Milton had attributed to the Fall God's command that

> his Angels turne ascanse
> The Poles of the Earth twice ten degrees and more
> From the Suns Axle,[59]

and just as Thomas Burnet in his *Sacred Theory of the Earth* had attributed the obliquity and the consequent variety of the seasons to the cataclysm responsible for the Flood, so Shelley writes that the thunder resulting from Prometheus' curse "made rock / The orbed world" [60] (I. 68–69) and that Earth refuses to repeat Prometheus' curse, lest Jupiter "link me to some wheel of pain / More torturing than the one whereon I roll" (I. 141–52). Since the earth's mere rotation about its own axis cannot justify the image of the torture-wheel, which,

[57] Note to *Queen Mab*, VI. 45, 46.   [58] *A Refutation of Deism.*
[59] *Paradise Lost*, X. 668–70.
[60] The source of the event, but not the significance Shelley assigns to it, is *Prometheus Bound* 1081.

incidentally, is also the instrument with which Jupiter punished Ixion, the reference to torture (*tortus:* "twisting") must be to the twisting motion resulting from the displacement of its axis from the perpendicular. Like the Fall of Man, Prometheus' curse—which, as we shall see, it represented in a variety of ways—has disordered nature and introduced all physical ills, not because God or (as Shelley had believed earlier) Necessity punishes man and nature in like manner, but because the universe is the mass of thoughts, including their various modes and combinations, in the One Mind. The consequences of the physicomental distortion are not only disease and natural cataclysms but also the extremes of the seasons described by Prometheus when, in his curse, he bade Jupiter "let alternate frost and fire / Eat into me" (I. 268–69) and by Asia when, among the ills of Jupiter's reign, she lists the "alternating shafts of frost and fire" of the "unseasonable seasons" (II. iv. 52–53). This loss of the Saturnian Age of perpetual spring as a consequence of the rocking of the earth is, moreover, precisely consonant with the Greco-Roman myth to which Shelley is committed. The Golden Age ended when Saturn was vanquished, the goddess of Justice fled, and the world came under the sway of Jupiter. Then, Ovid tells us, under the reign of Jupiter spring became but one of the four seasons, and the earth began to endure the extremes of burning heat and ice.[61]

---

[61] *Metamorphoses* i. 113–24. Dryden's translation, influenced by Ovid's commentators, brings these events into closer accord with astronomy:

> Then Summer, Autumn, Winter did appear;
> And Spring was but a season of the year.
> The sun his annual course obliquely made,
> Good days contracted, and enlarg'd the bad.
> Then air with sultry heats began to glow;
> The wings of winds were clogg'd with ice and snow.

It is, then, no stale metaphor but, in the philosophic context of the play, a richly appropriate fact that the moment initiating the restoration of Prometheus in Act II be the vernal equinox, when the obliquity is overcome and day and night are of equal length over the entire earth. The precession of the equinoxes, "though slow, being always in the same direction, and therefore continually accumulating, has early been remarked, and was the first of the celestial appearances that suggested the idea of an *annus magnus.*" [62] But Shelley's metaphysics, for reasons to be examined later, requires that Prometheus' restoration be abrupt and sudden, like that described by Shelley's friend John Frank Newton in a passage remarkably suggestive of Demogorgon's volcanic flight from beneath the earth:

> It is an astronomical fact which cannot easily be disputed, that the poles of the earth were at some distant period perpendicular to its orbit, as those of the planet Jupiter are now, whose inhabitants must therefore enjoy a perpetual spring.
>
> It was a tenet of the most ancient priests of whom we have any knowledge, the Brachmans, that still, by some portentous bursting forth of the earth's bowels, a second change will be accomplished, which shall bring back equal seasons and perpetual spring.[63]

Correspondingly, when Prometheus is at last restored, the renovation of Earth is represented in terms of a return to an eternal spring: through her "withered, old, and icy frame / The warmth of an immortal youth shoots down / Circling," and "In mild variety the seasons mild" clothe the entire world with "ever-living leaves,

[62] *Edinburgh Review,* XI (1808), 269–70.
[63] *The Return to Nature* (1821), in *The Pamphleteer,* XIX (1822), 506 and n. (first ed., 1811).

and fruits, and flowers" (III. iii. 88–90, 115, 123). All efforts to chart the strict chronology of *Prometheus Unbound* have invariably ended in frustration because, all this suggests, the various times of the day and their sequences are neither temporal in the usual sense nor even symbolic, but are actual conditions of the mind, to which all things are relative. It would be to no avail, for example, to ask whether an actual day passes between the morning of the vernal equinox opening Act II and the moment of Asia's reunion with Prometheus; the night that apparently intervenes is the darkness of Demogorgon's realm, the "lasting night" in which he wraps "heaven's kingless throne" (II. iv. 149). Now, not only were the dislocation and realignment of the earth's axis traditionally identified with the terminal points of the Platonic Great Year, which begins and ends with the vernal equinox; according to Pliny, among others, the exact moment of renewal is high noon—"Heaven's immortal noon," as Shelley names it in *Hellas* (223)—when all the heavenly bodies will again be in exact alignment.[64] Correspondingly, not only is Prometheus released with the arrival of spring, but the Hour that bears Asia to the freed Prometheus calls attention to the fact that she will rest from the labors of her flight "at noon" (II. iv. 172) and that on this day of restoration and renewal "The sun will rise not until noon" (II. v. 10), for at that perfect moment the new Promethean age will have begun.

Furthermore, if we now ask who brought about the distortion of the world and all its "physical" confusion, we are once again driven by the workings of the drama

---

[64] Pliny *Natural History* x. 2. 5. See also Albert R. Cirillo, "Noon-Midnight and the Temporal Structure of *Paradise Lost*," *ELH*, XXIX (1962), 372–95.

to the conclusion that Jupiter is but the privative mode of Prometheus, the One Mind. In his curse Prometheus calls down on himself all of Jupiter's tortures:

> Rain then thy plagues upon me here,
> Ghastly disease, and frenzying fear;
> And let alternate frost and fire
> Eat into me, and be thine ire
> Lightning, and cutting hail . . . ;
>
> (I. 266–70)

and these words, together with other descriptions in Act I of physical disorders, echo the defiance of Zeus by Aeschylus' Prometheus:

> Therefore let the lightning's forked curl be cast upon my head and let the sky be convulsed with thunder and the wrack of savage winds; let the hurricane shake the earth from its rooted base, and let the waves of the sea mingle with their savage surge the courses of the stars in heaven.[65]

Aeschylus' play then ends with Zeus visiting upon nature the cataclysms Prometheus had invoked. But it is a calculated aspect of Shelley's drama that he be far less exact about the agent of these events. Asia will explain that when, prior to his rebellion, Prometheus first gave Jupiter power, there came disease and the "unseasonable seasons" with "alternating shafts of frost and fire"; and she connects the two events only loosely (II. iv. 43–58). Earth places the cataclysms after Jupiter's thunder had enchained Prometheus, and she is equally vague about their immediate cause (I. 161–73). On the other hand, Earth also implies that Jupiter caused her distorted motion because of Prometheus' curse (I. 140–42); and yet Prometheus asserts that the words of his own curse, like a spell, "had power" that disrupted all nature and were

[65] *Prometheus Bound* 1043–50.

themselves a "thunder" that "made rock / The orbed world" (I. 61–69). But these last words derive from Aeschylus' play, where, significantly, it is Zeus, not Prometheus, who makes the earth rock in response to Prometheus' invocation of his tortures; [66] and the thunder which Shelley's Prometheus attributes to his curse is Jupiter's traditional instrument, not Prometheus'.[67] These varying accounts of the cause of nature's distortion arise, then, not from any confusion, but from the ambiguity built into the metaphysics of the poem. Nature is disordered because the One Mind is disordered, the distinction between the two being unreal. Hence the distortion is equally attributable to the One Mind's yielding up its powers, to the binding of the One Mind that necessarily results from this abdication, and to the curse of hate against the yielded powers that perpetuates the tyranny. And it is a matter of indifference whether the One Mind in its state of error and hate or whether "the supreme Tyrant" be considered the cause of the destruction of nature's Golden Age, for Jupiter is but the distorted reflection of Prometheus, "the shade from his own soul upthrown" so that it fills heaven and darkens earth.

Finally, the coherent dialogue in Act I between Earth and Prometheus that takes place, paradoxically, despite the total absence of communication between the speakers must also be examined in the light of Shelley's brand of idealism. Earth and her elements, notwithstanding Prometheus' plea, refuse to repeat Prometheus' curse because to do so, Earth explains, would be to employ a language intelligible not only to Prometheus but also to Jupiter, who would torture her more severely than when he first heard the curse. Earth and her components,

---

[66] *Ibid.*, 1081.
[67] Contrast *Prometheus Unbound*, I. 162: ". . . his [Jupiter's] thunder chained thee here."

therefore, must be able to speak two different languages, Prometheus and Jupiter only one of the two. Thereafter Earth and Prometheus exchange a series of speeches and respond to each other with what appears to the reader to be mutual understanding, even though it is explicit that Earth is employing a language unintelligible to Prometheus. To him the words of the mountains, springs, air, and whirlwind are only "a sound of voices: not the voice / Which I gave forth" on uttering the curse (I. 112–13); and Earth's "inorganic voice" is but "an awful whisper . . . scarce like sound" (I. 132–33) that affects him and notifies him of her presence but does not communicate intelligible thoughts. Earth's speech works strangely on him:

> Obscurely thro' my brain, like shadows dim,
> Sweep awful thoughts, rapid and thick. I feel
> Faint, like one mingled in entwining love;
> Yet 'tis not pleasure. (I. 146–49)

Nevertheless, even Earth is aware that she is speaking in a tongue unknown to him. Obviously, the reader is being asked to entertain a complex and paradoxical dramatic hypothesis. Of course only a single language is available to Shelley and his reader, and yet the reader must accept the explicit statement that Earth's language is really different from Prometheus'. And although Prometheus questions and answers Earth as though their communication were complete, the reader must assume that Prometheus is in fact speaking a soliloquy which, quite by chance, happens to form a coherent dialogue with Earth:

> *Prometheus.* . . .
> . . . .
> Speak, Spirit! from thine inorganic voice
> I only know that thou art moving near

And love. How cursed I him?
The Earth.   How canst thou hear
Who knowest not the language of the dead?
Prometheus. Thou art a living spirit; speak as they.
The Earth. I dare not speak like life. . . .   (I. 135–40)

Shelley's rejection of materialism and the dualism of mind and matter must have driven him to reconsider the function of language, for he could no longer assume it to be an analysis of percepts into the components and relationships obtaining among their counterparts in an outside reality. It is clear that he was frequently inclined to examine the implications of the intellectual philosophy in grammatical terms and hence to conceive of linguistic structures as imprecise, artificial expedients for organizing thoughts and as only metaphoric of the relationships that truly exist in the mind. [68] The personal pronouns he found to be "grammatical devices invented simply for arrangement, and totally devoid of the intense and exclusive sense usually attached to them"; [69] and the various tenses, he decided, really express the changing modes of the existence of our percepts relative to ourselves.[70] As other empiricists and idealists were driven by their premises to recognize, language does not report the structure of an external universe; it is a conventional arrangement imposing an arbitrary analytical structure on thought, even though thought is not truly divisible into components.[71] Instead of reporting forms, it is formative. When properly exploited by man as a particulariz-

[68] His order of a copy of Lord Monboddo's *On the Origin and Progress of Language* is evidence of his interest in linguistic theory (letter to Clio Rickman, 24 Dec. 1812). His *Speculations on Metaphysics* also shows his knowledge of John Horn Tooke's philological writings.
[69] *On Life.*   [70] *Speculations on Metaphysics.*
[71] Robert L. Politzer has shown how an acceptance of Berkeley's idealism led Maupertuis into a kind of pre-Humboldtian linguistic relativism that claims that a conventional linguistic system structures knowledge ("On the Linguistic Philosophy of Maupertuis and Its Relation to the History

ing and relational system, language defines and organizes otherwise vague and chaotic thoughts:

> Language is a perpetual Orphic song,
> Which rules with Daedal harmony a throng
> Of thoughts and forms, which else senseless and shape-
> less were.
>
> (IV. 415–17)

Later, in his *Defence of Poetry,* Shelley was to write that "language is arbitrarily produced by the imagination and has relation to thoughts alone" and that it expresses the relational and unifying principles of the mind, not the order of "objects and the impressions represented by them." Indeed, since the universe is constituted of our "mass of knowledge . . . , including our own nature," the structure of the universe is determined for the human mind by the way in which a linguistic system shapes (in Shelley's terminology, "creates") our knowledge, or thought: "speech created thought, / Which is the measure of the universe" (II. iv. 72–73). Yet it must be understood that all this applies only to the human mind, together with its illusions of distinct minds, distinct thoughts, time, space, and the distinction between subject and object. Given these illusions, the relational power of language can be employed to weave a "Daedal harmony," an organic order that tends to overcome the chaos of human thoughts. But language is both a blessing and a frustration. Even under the compulsion of the human mind's extraordinary apprehensions of perfect unity, language can never entirely overcome discreteness

---

of Linguistic Relativism," *Symposium,* XVII [1963], 5–16). He also instances J. D. Michaelis' *Beantwortung der Frage von dem Einflusz der Meinungen auf die Sprache und der Sprache auf die Meinungen* (1759) and J. G. Sulzer's *Observations sur l'influence reciproque de la raison sur le langage et du langage sur la raison* (1767).

and the dimensions of mutability because man cannot overcome his illusory state that is the necessary condition for his existence as man; and when Shelley aspires to express the absolute unity of being, he can only lament,

> The winged words on which my soul would pierce
> Into the height of Love's rare Universe,
> Are chains of lead around its flight of fire,[72]

or complain, "These words inefficient and metaphorical. Most words so—No help!" [73]

The distinction Earth draws in her paradoxical "dialogue" with Prometheus is that her language is known only to mortals and therefore not to Prometheus, who is immortal. Hers is "the language of the dead" (I. 138), understandable only "to those who die" (I. 151); and even at the end of the Promethean action, upon being questioned by Asia about those "who die," she answers in words almost identical with those of her earlier explanation (I. 148–51):

> It would avail not to reply:
> Thou art immortal, and this tongue is known
> But to the uncommunicating dead.
>
> (III. iii. 110–12)

Earth, then, can belong to mortality or, being potentially a "living spirit," to immortality; Prometheus, like his distorted shadow Jupiter, to immortality alone. The distinction is between life and death, and the key term is "living spirit." Clearly "life" here does not refer to human existence: as Earth explains, "Death is the veil which those who live call life: / They sleep, and it is lifted" (III. iii. 113–14). Mortality lives a death; and what it calls death

---

[72] *Epipsychidion,* 588–90.   [73] *On Love.*

is really its removal. Instead, "life" is to be understood in the sense that Shelley assigned it in his essay on that subject, the identity of being and perception, the unity of mind and the universe, subject and object. As the One Mind, Prometheus can understand only the language of "life." It is also a language available to Earth because, assumed in Mind, she can be a "living spirit"; or, conceived of as divorced from Mind and subjected to the mutability and dimensions of mortality, she can appear as those thoughts illusorily considered to be "external objects." We are to understand, therefore, that in her dialogue with Prometheus Earth speaks the language of mankind, which postulates the illusory distinction between earth and mind. Dividing herself from Mind as an external thing, Earth cannot speak the curse, which is an expression of Mind, and her words appear to Prometheus only as "an awful whisper," only as obscure thoughts. Despite Prometheus' awareness of the love that, were it complete, would unite him with Earth, he is conscious of the division effected by the mortal language that separates mind from an external world: "I only know that thou art moving near / And love" (I. 136–37). The ontological division, moreover, must also be a moral one, since the distinction between metaphysics and ethics is unreal. As the mere mass of thoughts called external and falsely filtered out of "life," Earth continues to meditate Prometheus' curse "In secret joy and hope" (I. 184), erroneously believing that the Mind's hate-filled resistance will ultimately overcome Jupiter. Related to Prometheus only as "things" are supposedly related to mortal minds, Earth misunderstands the moral significance of Prometheus' retraction of the curse, just as Urania, being the spirit of earthly life, fails to understand the true significance of Adonais' postmortal existence. Divorced from

Mind and therefore from moral truth, Earth can conceive of Prometheus' repentance only as defeat, and not as the removal of the impediment to Jupiter's overthrow:

> Howl, Spirits of the living and the dead,
> Your refuge, your defence lies fallen and vanquished.
>
> (I. 310–11)

CHAPTER II

✌ MYTH ☙

MAN's works of art, according to Prometheus, are

> the mediators
> Of that best worship love, by him and us
> Given and returned,
>
> (III. iii. 58–60)

and we shall have deeper insight into Shelley's artistry if
we can understand how poetry mediates between the
human mind and the One Mind, that is, between mutable
diversity and division on the one hand and the immutable unity of absolute being on the other. Now, in his *Defence of Poetry* Shelley's radical principle of art appears
under such various synonyms as "order," "arrangement,"
"combination," "relation," "harmony," and "rhythm." [1]
By building a value system predicated upon an Absolute,
not of being, but of form, Shelley conceived of the True,
the Beautiful, and the Good as but differently biased
views of this ineffably unitary form. Consequently, the
differences among artists, teachers, "institutors of laws,"

---

[1] In my "Shelley's Last Poetics: A Reconsideration" (in *From Sensibility to Romanticism*, ed. F. W. Hillis and H. Bloom, pp. 487–511), I
have attempted to analyse Shelley's poetic theory in full and am here
drawing on that analysis.

[54]

"founders of civil society," and "inventors of the arts of life" are limited to the differences among the media in which each seeks to express his extraordinary apprehension of "this indestructible order." Each medium of expression, whether language or social action, for example, has its own peculiar highest order or rhythm, recognizable by its providing the highest pleasure of which the medium is capable, and falling short of the ideal unity only because of the clogs inherent in the materials. Poetry, therefore, "reproduces all that it represents," which is to say that it reorganizes all the material that it imitates; or, as Shelley expressed the same idea in the Preface to *Prometheus Unbound*, the products of the poet "are beautiful and new, not because the portions of which they are composed had no previous existence in the mind of man or in nature, but because the whole produced by their combination has some intelligible and beautiful analogy with those sources of emotion and thought. . . ."

It follows from these principles that for Shelley the imagination is entirely a combinatory, or organizing, power and that the determinant of poetry is the organic configuration into which the poet excites his materials, its perfection being proportional to its formal approximation to the intuited One which subsumes absolute Beauty, Truth, and Goodness. Given our imperfect mortal existence, wherein all things and thoughts are necessarily discrete, the poet's essential creative task is to interweave the discrete to form a beautiful whole, although the criterion and motive of the beautiful wholeness must be an extraordinary intuition of absolute unity, which is beyond expression because all distinctions, and therefore all relationships, dissolve into it. The laws, or principles, whereby the poet effects this organic

[55]

order are not those discovered in the perceived relationships among events or objects: poetry is not a picture of the structure of perceptions but the creative expression of the mind, and all expression, as opposed to impression, is "subject to the laws of that from which it proceeds." A mere representation of perceptions according to their perceived arrangements is a "catalogue of detached facts, which have no other bond of connexion than time, place, circumstance, cause and effect" and therefore, being a display of "appearances" only, is a "mirror which obscures and distorts that which should be beautiful." On the contrary, the laws that interweave elemental thoughts into an organic wholeness aspiring to the absolute form of the One are, like Kantian categories, the mind's own associative laws of "equality, diversity, unity,[2] contrast, mutual dependence." In short, the elements of poetry are thoughts, all of which derive ultimately from perception; and these thoughts the poet's imagination, excited by apprehension of the absolute and inexpressible form, composes according to the mind's own connective laws into "other thoughts, each containing within itself the principle of its own integrity." Containing within itself the principle whereby it is whole, the poem is self-sustaining and thus is released from time, place, and circumstance.

The Absolute which is Truth-Beauty-Goodness and which is the goal toward which poetry aspires is not to be confused with the One Mind that Prometheus represents. The One Mind, we have already observed, accounts for being, not values. Obviously, *Prometheus Unbound* is concerned primarily with ethical perfection,

---

[2] What Shelley meant by wholeness of form is vividly suggested by his having written "flowing together" in the manuscript of the *Defence* before substituting "unity" (Bodleian MS Shelley adds. d.1).

[56]

but the ultimate source of that perfection and its compelling energy, although we may consider it assumed in
the drama, is not brought onto the stage as a dramatic
character or as part of the action. The One which is
Truth-Beauty-Goodness is, however, the thematic center
not only of such religious poems as *Hymn to Intellectual
Beauty* and *Adonais* but also of Shelley's poetics, especially as it is formulated in his *Defence of Poetry;* for the
One, so conceived, not only is absolute form but is itself
actively organizational, molding everything "into the
nearest arrangement possible to the perfect archetype." [3]
It is "one Spirit vast" that "With life and love makes
chaos ever new" [4] because its necessary character is to
model, "as they pass, all the elements of this mixed universe to the purest and most perfect shape which it belongs to their nature to assume," [5] just as every human
mode of expression, according to the *Defence,* has its
own highest order approximating the One. Whatever
receives this "perfect shape" becomes both an expression
and representation of Truth-Beauty-Goodness, for

> the one Spirit's plastic stress
> Sweeps through the dull dense world, compelling there,
> All new successions to the forms they wear;
> Torturing th' unwilling dross that checks its flight
> To its own likeness, as each mass may bear.
>
> (*Adonais,* 381–85)

This idea of a perfect shaping energy at work upon the
universe corresponds to Shelley's conception of the
poet's plastic imagination that molds his thoughts into
one self-sustaining thought. In at least one phase of his
speculations Shelley held that each human spirit is a

[3] *On the Devil and Devils.*   [4] *Ode to Liberty,* 88–89.
[5] *Essay on Christianity.*

derivative part of this "one Spirit" and will ultimately flow "Back to the burning fountain whence it came, / A portion of the Eternal" (*Adonais,* 339–40); and through this doctrine he had the means of attributing to the creative human mind an organizational power that is a portion of the perfect formative energy that acts upon the universe. Just as the One Spirit compels the elements of the world to a shape resembling its own unity, the human mind's sporadic intuitions of the One inspire the imagination to urge the mind's thoughts to the highest approximation of that form. Inspired by the perfect unity of Truth-Beauty-Goodness, art is the supreme human syntax and therefore mediates between man's mutable existence and absolute being.

The artistic processes of many of Shelley's poems are rooted in these principles. Perhaps the poetic action most profoundly determined by them is that of *Adonais,* in which the poet's plastic imagination, sweeping repeatedly over approximately the same complexes of images, compels them progressively through a series of false, imperfect orderings to their final perfect arrangement, which is the most beautiful form of which they are capable and, synonymously, the highest truth that they can embody and reveal.[6] For example, it proves imperfect to conceive of Keats's poems as "like flowers that mock the corse beneath," flowers with which the poet "had adorned and hid the coming bulk of death"; this arrangement of the images falls short of the highest unity, or beauty, of which they are capable, and therefore its implication that all things must end in annihilation falls short of the truth. Nor is it then adequate to believe that the only thing that persists is nature's vegetative anima-

[6] See my *The Subtler Language* (Baltimore, 1959), pp. 305–61.

tion, which passes through an endless cycle of death and rebirth:

> The leprous corpse touched by this spirit tender
> Exhales itself in flowers of gentle breath;
>   . . . they illumine death
> And mock the merry worm that wakes beneath.

Only the scene at the Protestant Cemetery reveals the beautiful truth that the spirit is immortal and that physical death is irrelevant. The spot is unrelated to the mortal, temporal world outside, where, as in the first arrangement of the images, "flowering weeds, and fragrant copses dress / The bones of Desolation's nakedness"; here, instead,

> like an infant's smile, over the dead,
> A light of laughing flowers along the grass is spread.

Only now have flowers, corpse, and light been drawn into the most nearly perfect interrelationship that they permit. Differently applied, the same poetic principles make clear why, in *The Sensitive Plant*, the sensory descriptions paint only the mutability and decay of the garden-world while the imagination, ordering the very same images into metaphors and visions, compels that world to assume the shape of a mirror image of the eternal heavens. The illusive senses, that is, perceiving only according to the inorganic and transient arrangement of impressions, perceive images in their mutable relationships; the plastic imagination shapes them into their eternal proportions. For the imagination is—as Shelley considered himself to be—a revolutionist and reformer, first shaking "Thought's stagnant chaos" (IV. 380) and then striving to rearrange the liberated elements into the same formal perfection of Truth-Beauty-Goodness as does the plastic stress of the One Spirit. Employing the integrative laws of mental association and transcending the mutable relationships communicated by the senses, the poetic imagination shatters false and imperfect arrangements of thought and reconstitutes those thoughts according to the indestructible organization they ought to have.

In *Prometheus Unbound* this doctrine of the workings and purpose of the plastic imagination is responsible for the transformation and syncretism of the myths that constitute the body of the drama. Thomas Love Peacock reports that Shelley once commented on Spenser's giant who holds the scales and wishes to "rectify the physical and moral evils which result from inequality of condition."[7] Artegall, Shelley explained, "argues with the Giant; the Giant has the best of the argument; Artegall's iron man knocks him over into the sea and drowns him. This is the usual way in which power deals with opinion." When Peacock objected that this is not the lesson Spenser intended, Shelley replied, "Perhaps not; it is the lesson which he conveys to me. I am of the Giant's faction."[8] In the giant's intention to reduce all things "unto equality" Spenser saw the impending dissolution of hierarchy and the return to chaos; from Shelley's point of view this was the wrong conception of order and therefore the wrong ordering of the mythic details embodying it, for what to Spenser was necessary superiority and subordination was to republican Shelley the frustration of all possibility of perfect unity. The occasion for Peacock's note was a reference in one of Shelley's letters to

[7] *Peacock's Memoirs of Shelley*, ed. H. F. B. Brett-Smith (London, 1909), p. 162n.
[8] Peacock adds that Shelley also "held that the Enchanter in the first canto [of Thomson's *Castle of Indolence*] was a true philanthropist, and the Knight of Arts and Industry in the second an oligarchical impostor overthrowing truth by power" (*ibid.*).

Artegall's giant, introduced, significantly, as a comment on the recently completed Act I of *Prometheus Unbound:* the act, Shelley writes, is an attempt to "cast what weight I can into the right scale of that balance which the Giant (of Arthegall) holds." [9] For egalitarian Shelley was engaged in reforming and reinterpreting the myth of god-fearing Aeschylus at least as radically as he did that of Spenser, the defender of hierarchism, and to the same end of perfect order. Recasting that myth into the shape and proportions that, according to his imaginative vision, it ought to have as the highest unity of which its components are capable meant to Shelley not only the achievement of the highest formal beauty but also—since it amounts to the same thing—the purging of error and the attainment of truth.

To Shelley myth is not fanciful fable. Whatever its genesis, it is not mistaken for external fact, and therefore it is more truly real than the sensory world that man falsely believes to reside outside his mind. Since "things" exist for man only in the form of thoughts, the elements organized by the poet are thoughts recognized as wholly mental and not mistaken for any independent externality. The thoughts composed by the imagination are those upon which the mind has already acted "so as to color them with its own light," [10] which is a reflection of the light of the perfect One. Or, as Shelley expresses the same idea in *Prometheus Unbound,* the poet does not heed objects as external "things," but first watches the "lake-reflected sun illume" them and then organizes ("creates") these transfigured thoughts into "forms more real than living man, / Nurslings of immortality!" (I. 744–49). The elements of myth, being unmistakably

[9] Letter to Peacock [23–24 Jan. 1819] (*Letters,* ed. Jones, II, 71).
[10] *Defence of Poetry.*

[61]

mental interpretations of "things," are pre-eminently thoughts and therefore pre-eminently the valid materials to which the poet is obliged to give the "purest and most perfect shape."

But if the constituent details of myths are especially real for Shelley, it follows that the component elements of one myth are as valid as those of any other, since they are all thoughts and therefore indiscriminately available to the mythopoeic poet. Syncretic mythology had been revitalized in the eighteenth century, especially by those deists who, arguing for the common basis of all faiths, had attempted to demonstrate the interconvertibility of all myths.[11] This tradition of syncretism was part of Shelley's intellectual heritage, and his mentalistic ontology provided it with a special philosophic justification. If, then, all mythic elements, from Jupiter to King Bladud, are real and valid, the various received myths are not to be thought of as discrete narratives or distinct national faiths, but only as variant efforts of the mind to apprehend the same truth; and hence the stuff of all such myths is, indifferently, available to the poet for his task of compelling thoughts to their most nearly perfect structure. Indeed, directly after announcing to Peacock the completion of the first act of his mythopoeic drama and directly before his idiosyncratic interpretation of Artegall's giant, Shelley wrote that he could conceive of a "great work," not of poetry but of moral and political science, "embodying the discoveries of all ages, & harmonizing the contending creeds by which mankind have been ruled." For it is Shelley's assumption that if all creeds, or their mythic embodiments, were shaped into the highest form they admit, they would be precisely

[11] See Albert J. Kuhn, "English Deism and the Development of Romantic Mythological Syncretism," *PMLA*, LXXI (1956), 1094–1116.

translatable into each other. Despite his modest dis-
claimer—"Far from me is such an attempt"—the syncretism of this "great work" is at the heart of *Prometheus
Unbound*.

Moreover, given Shelley's interpretation of "thought,"
it follows that empirical science, folk science, legends,
and all literature that has been assimilated as an operative part of human culture are also mental configurations
of thoughts that recognize the mental nature of "things";
and therefore they, at least as much as conventional
myths, are also permanently real in the sense that supposedly objective things are not. Consequently, all these
thoughts, too, are among the materials for the poet's imagination to syncretize and interlock into the most nearly
perfect form. *Adonais,* for example, is not merely another
variant of the Venus and Adonis myth; it recasts that
myth into a new and presumably true system of interre-
lationships, but it also organically integrates the re-
formed myth with the ancient belief that souls derive
from stars, with astronomy scientific and fabular, with
the science of optics, and with various traditional metaphors and symbols, all of them having the same kind and
degree of eternal reality because they are the mind's
conceptions, rather than perceptions, of things. Myth so
inclusively defined is not an assemblage of accepted fictional terms supporting an accretion of rich connota-
tions, as it was for Dryden and Pope; nor merely a fiction
that reveals truth better than facts; nor an upsurging
from the unconscious. Its components are indestructible
and eternal mental possessions. Consequently, however
diverse and unrelated their traditional contexts, they ask,
like all other thoughts, to be interwoven into a beautiful
whole "containing within itself the principle of its own
integrity." If the structures of given myths are already

beautiful and true, Shelley held, they are integral thoughts having "the power of attracting and assimilating to their own nature all other thoughts," [12] and thus any conventional myth so organized is inexhaustibly capable of rendering truths for a poet by giving its shape to them. On the other hand, since error, ugliness, and evil are but various modes of disorder, the task of the imagination is to reform erroneous, misshapen myths according to the model of the mind's extraordinary apprehensions of perfect unity.

II

Such a conception of myth and the function of the imagination entails an especially ambiguous relation between the traditional form of a legend or myth and the poet's use of it, and demands of the reader an equally ambiguous frame of mind. When, in his *Rape of the Lock,* Pope calls Thalestris to Belinda's aid, the mere appearance of this queen of the Amazons tacitly attaches to Belinda the unnatural displacement in the sexual hierarchy, the belligerent rejection of men, and the Amazonian ideal of a self-sufficient female society, just as Pope's casting Clarissa's advice in the form of Sarpedon's speech seriocomically elevates that advice to heroic stature and demands of Belinda quasi-heroic deeds. Through knowledge already in the reader's mind, traditional qualities and meanings outside the poem attach themselves to elements in the poem. Or, for ironic purposes, the likening of Belinda's apotheosized lock to Berenice's evokes the reader's knowledge that Catullus' Berenice sacrificed her hair that her husband might be

[12] *Defence of Poetry.*

returned to her, and the clash between that intimated fact outside the poem and Belinda's rejection of the Baron within the poem is at the center of what the poem is saying. In either kind of instance the established structures of the myths upon which Pope draws are operative in the poem by allusion, and the reader, when called upon, must make them present that they may perform upon the text their acts of supplying, amplifying, and complicating significances. But according to the implications of Shelley's theory the myths that appear in his poetry, however traditional, are to be understood as really having no inherited contexts at all. As either actually or potentially true-beautiful organizations of thought, they are universal and eternal forms that become limited in proportion as they are thought of as specific myths; and any particular previous appearance of the myth is not a locus for literary allusion but merely another instance of the real or potential archetypal form.

For example, the myth of Aurora, goddess of the dawn, and her union with the beautiful mortal, Tithonus, is recognizable behind Shelley's account of the creation of works of art:

> And lovely apparitions, dim at first,
> Then radiant, as the mind, arising bright
> From the embrace of beauty, whence the forms
> Of which these are the phantoms, casts on them
> The gathered rays which are reality.
>
> (III. iii. 49–53)

Yet in the more important sense the myth is not present at all behind the symbols of dawn and light, which are themselves adequate to incorporate the meaning; and although the myth does provide an additional propriety to the word "embrace," Shelley certainly does nothing to evoke the myth as an efficient reverberating echo. The

Aurora myth is not to be understood as a particular narrative generally current in Western culture; it is the mind's composition of thoughts into an integral and self-sustaining thought that, because of its beauty and truth as a composition, has here assimilated to its own form another body of thoughts—or, rather, has given its form to a body of thoughts and thus lost its own special identity. Awareness of the myth will allow the reader to recognize the patterning source; and yet the end product of this recognition is, paradoxically, that he think as though no myth were present, but only the perfect archetypal arrangement, of which the story of Aurora and Tithonus is a limited instance. Of the same order of mythopoeia is Shelley's adaptation of the legend of King Bladud, the mythical founder of Bath, who stumbled upon the curative hot springs when, a banished leper, he followed one of his afflicted swine, and whose dramatic return after his cure enraptured his mother.[13] Hate, fear, and pain, Shelley writes, are to

> Leave Man, even as a leprous child is left,
> Who follows a sick beast to some warm cleft
> Of rocks, through which the might of healing springs is
>   poured;
> Then when it wanders home with rosy smile,
> Unconscious, and its mother fears awhile
> It is a spirit, then, weeps on her child restored.
>
>   (IV. 388–93)

Although this is Bladud's legendary history in every detail, the poet's refusal to call it into conscious attention makes present only a beautiful pattern, not a special al-

---

[13] The allusion has been pointed out by G. M. Matthews, "Shelley's Grasp upon the Actual," *Essays in Criticism,* IV (1954), 329. The legend is recorded in full in Richard Warner's *History of Bath* (Bath, 1801).

lusion. Nor is the term "thought-executing," borrowed from *King Lear,* deposited in the following speech by Prometheus with the design of calling up some functional reaction between the plot of *Lear* and the relation of Jupiter to Prometheus:

> Evil minds
> Change good to their own nature. I gave all
> He [Jupiter] has; and in return he chains me here
> Years, ages, night and day . . .
> . . . .
> Whilst my beloved race is trampled down
> By his thought-executing ministers.
> Such is the tyrant's recompense: 'tis just:
> He who is evil can receive no good;
> And for a world bestowed, or a friend lost,
> He can feel hate, fear, shame; not gratitude:
> He but requites me for his own misdeed.
> Kindness to such is keen reproach, which breaks
> With bitter stings the light sleep of Revenge.
> Submission, thou dost know I cannot try.[14]
>
> (I. 380–95)

An interpretation of Lear's relation to his daughters is, I think, present formally and yet otherwise inoperative; it is present for the poet—and the critic—not for the "pure" reader that the play hypothesizes, who is to experience the work as though it exists in total independence and autonomy. The assumption behind the creative act is that Shakespeare formed a beautiful and true arrangement of thoughts, and Shelley is fulfilling his doctrine that such mythic orderings are always capable of attracting to their shape other truths; but he is not engaging

---

[14] The basis of this speech, but not of its form or thematic elaboration, is *Prometheus Bound* 223–27.

Shakespeare's play in his text to illuminate it or to complicate and thicken its meaning. These are, admittedly, extreme examples of Shelley's assimilation of myths as archetypal orderings, but they are symptomatic of his mythopoeic methods and indicate the paradoxical informed ignorance they demand for the most complete reading.

We have seen, however, that Shelley conceives of the poet as not merely an assimilator of beautiful mythic forms: inasmuch as he is creative, he is a mythopoeist, not by inventing myths, but by reconstituting the imperfect ones that already exist. His creations are "beautiful and new, not because the portions of which they are composed had no previous existence in the mind of man or in nature," but because of "the whole produced by their combination." Indeed, just as Shelley held that all human minds are portions of the One Mind, so he believed that, because of the interconnection and interdependence of all poems, each is a fragment of, or partial movement toward, "that great poem which all poets, like the co-operating thoughts of one great mind, have built up since the beginning of the world." [15] Evidence of his respect for this position is to be found not only in his resort to traditional materials but even in his refraining from forging new links to regroup and interrelate diverse myths; for his implicit assumption is that the true and beautiful relationships of wholeness already exist potentially in the qualities of the given materials, waiting to be properly drawn out. Consequently, he rather strictly confines himself to the inherent syntactical potentials, however minor or neglected they may be in the conventional myths, and his mythopoeic art lies especially in eliciting and exploiting these potentials to form new combinations.

[15] *Defence of Poetry.*

Although the wife assigned to Prometheus by the traditional myth and by Aeschylus was the Oceanid Hesione, Shelley had authority in Herodotus for wedding him to Asia instead; and yet the substitution did not violate or sacrifice any of Hesione's characteristics, for according to Apollodorus, Hesiod, and other theogonists, Asia was also an Oceanid, born of Tethys and Oceanus. Shelley, therefore, could invent two sisters for Asia—Panthea and Ione—and properly substitute them for Aeschylus' chorus of Oceanids. This mythologically legitimate substitution allows him to integrate into the body of the drama what in Aeschylus is a dramatically separate group of commentators on the action, yet without losing the power to use Panthea and Ione as commentators. But in addition, not only Asia's oceanic origin but also her quasi-geographic name, unlike Hesione's, opened up the possibility of investing her with the character and symbolic values of the sea-born Aphrodite. Like the Oceanids, Aphrodite was born of the seminal sea; and, striking a mean between the Cytherean and the Cyprian waters whence, according to the two different traditions, Aphrodite arose, Shelley locates Asia's sea-birth near the land of her name, Asia Minor, and describes it in the conventional terms of that of Aphrodite Anadyomene:

> The Nereids tell
> That on the day when the clear hyaline
> Was cloven at thy uprise, and thou didst stand
> Within a veined shell, which floated on
> Over the calm floor of the crystal sea,
> Among the Egean isles, and by the shores
> Which bear thy name; love . . .
> . . . .
> Burst from thee. . . .
>
> (II. v. 20–28)

Similarly, at the apocalyptic climax of the play, when Asia undergoes a second spiritual birth and again radiates the light of love, she is borne to Prometheus, as she was brought ashore on her first birth, in the shell which is Venus' symbol (II. iv. 157). Mary Shelley, of course, was right to call her "the same as Venus," [16] and Asia's Venus-like character is consistently sustained throughout the drama, for she is to perform a role somewhat like that of the Venus-Lady of *The Sensitive Plant,* who tends a garden like that of Adonis. The Platonic distinction between the heavenly and earthly Venuses customary in discussions of Shelley seems to me quite beside the point and will be neglected here. Asia's nature is to radiate love, and her separation from Prometheus is the absence of love: "Most vain all hope but love; and thou art far, / Asia!" (I. 808–9). But there are no categories or levels of love in the poem, and Asia is the love divorced from the One Mind when it is enchained by its own dark tyrannical shadow, the love reunited with the One Mind when it wills its own freedom. She is the ideal condition of Being. But Being, or the One Mind, is also the "living" spirit in that ideally it is the identity of perceiver and perception; and Shelley is everywhere inclined to conceive of life (in this ideal sense) and love —and light—as intimately related and nearly synonymous, animation being the luminous energy and joy of love. For example, Shelley writes of "one Spirit vast," the plastic force that "With life and love makes chaos ever new"; and Beatrice Cenci laments that she is cut off "from the only world I know, / From light, and life, and love." [17] Even the reanimated spring vegetation, in

---

[16] Note to *Prometheus Unbound.* No evidence, however, has been found to support her statement that this identification had been made by other mythologists; and her identification of Asia as "Nature" is not especially helpful, although that term does apply to the traditional Venus Genetrix.
[17] *Ode to Liberty,* 88–89; *Cenci,* V. iv. 85–86.

"diffusing" its scent and color, is spending, "in love's delight, / The beauty and the joy" of its renewed vital-
ity.[18] Hence the love that Asia radiates "like the atmosphere / Of the sun's fire filling the living world" (II. v.
26–27) is also a life-giving power; and Shelley can remain consistent with his mythic données because Venus
—Lucretius' *alma Venus*—is also the generative spirit
like Asia, the Venus-Lady of *The Sensitive Plant*, and the
Venus Urania of *Adonais*. Just as flowers burst into
bloom and grass sprang up at the touch of Aphrodite's
feet when she first walked on the shores,[19] so Asia's
"footsteps pave the world / With loveliness" (II. i. 68–
69), and her presence generates life in the barren Indian
vale of her exile,

> rugged once
> And desolate and frozen . . . ;
> But now invested with fair flowers and herbs,
> And haunted by sweet airs and sounds, which flow
> Among the woods and waters, from the ether
> Of her transforming presence, which would fade
> If it were mingled not with thine [Prometheus'].
>
> (I. 827–33)

For life-love obviously is as dependent upon Mind for its
existence as Earth is, and presumably the spirits of Prometheus and Asia, despite their separation, remain related through the agency of Panthea and Ione. It is,
then, in accord with Asia's Venus-role that in the lyric
concluding Act II this "Lamp of Earth" and "Child of
Light" be addressed as "Life of Life" (II. v. 58), the love
which is the essence of life and therefore of Being; and
that Prometheus speak of once "drinking life" from Asia's

[18] *Adonais,* 170–71. See also *Queen Mab,* VIII. 108; *Revolt of Islam,* IX.
xxx. 1; *To* —— ("When passion's trance"), 15; *The Magnetic Lady to
Her Patient,* 21.
[19] Hesiod *Theogony* 194; Lucretius, i. 7ff. Compare *Adonais,* 208–16.

"loved eyes" (I. 123), since love's power is traditionally located in the light of the eyes. We can take literally the belief of Shelley's Rosalind that "life was love" and can understand why it is more than merely high praise that in Lionel, who represents Shelley himself, "love and life . . . were twins, / Born at one birth . . . children of one mother." [20]

It is proper, therefore, that Asia make her first appearance in the drama at the opening of Act II with the very moment of the advent of the physicospiritual spring, the moment of renovation made possible by the One Mind's retraction of the curse. For spring, and, more particularly, the month of April that introduces spring, was sacred to Venus as goddess of generation. The reanimating spring is a property of Asia's symbolic nature as a condition of Mind; and because Venus was traditionally attended and prepared by the Hour (Hora) of spring,[21] it is consonant with the general structure of the conventional myth that at the end of Act II Asia ascend from Demogorgon's realm in the chariot of that Hour who is a "young spirit" with "eyes of hope" (II. iv. 159–60) and that this same vernal Hour, "most desired" and "more loved and lovely / Than all thy sisters" (III. iii. 69–70), also be appointed to convey the destined renewal to the entire earth and to mortal man and so bring the Promethean action to its fulfillment.

The Spirit of the Earth who appears in Acts III and IV also derives from the network of interconnected myths introduced into the drama by the identification of Asia with Venus. For this winged child, patronizingly addressed as "wayward" and "wanton" and marked by suggestively sexual speech, obviously performs in the

---

[20] *Rosalind and Helen*, 765, 622–25.
[21] E.g., Pindar *Nemean* viii. 1; and *Homeric Hymn to Venus*.

poem's special context the role of Eros, or Cupid, son of Venus. Like the mythic Eros, to whom so many different parents were assigned that his ancestry was notoriously uncertain,[22] the Spirit of the Earth knows not "whence it sprung," although it addresses the Venus-like Asia as "Mother, dearest mother" (III. iv. 23–24). Related in this manner to Asia, "Lamp of Earth," "Child of Light," and personification of Love, from whose loved eyes Prometheus once drank life, the winged Spirit of the Earth, like the Eros from whom he derives, carries a torch and thereby becomes part of the symbolic complex of eyes, light, and love. "This is my torch-bearer," says Earth to Asia,

> Who let his lamp out in old time with gazing
> On eyes from which he kindled it anew
> With love, which is as fire, sweet daughter mine,
> For such is that within thine own.
>
> (III. iii. 148–52)

This conceit further identifies the Spirit of the Earth with Eros; for when Tibullus wrote that fierce Love lights his twin torches from Sulpicia's eyes when he would inflame the gods, he gave birth to a persistent motif in the descriptions of the god of love.[23] As the son of Venus-Asia, therefore, the Eros-like Spirit is a derivative portion of love-life-light that in the final acts performs as the infused spirit of earth and there replaces Earth herself in the drama. First introduced by Earth as her "torch-bearer," he is instructed to guide the Promethean company to the destined cave, just as the classical

---

[22] E.g., Plato *Symposium* 178; *Greek Anthology* v. 177.
[23] Tibullus iv. 2. 5–6. For some instances of Tibullus' conceit, see *The Elegies of Albius Tibullus*, ed. Kirby Flower Smith (New York, 1913), pp. 488–89, and M. B. Ogle, "The Classical Origin and Tradition of Literary Conceits," *American Journal of Philology*, XXXIV (1913), 133–35.

Eros, whose torch was also kindled with "love, which is as fire," lighted lovers on the way to their union; and thereafter this Spirit "guides the earth thro' heaven" (III. iv. 7). This last transformation is especially apt, since the Intelligences that, according to Plato, move the heavenly spheres were converted by Platonized Christianity into angels, and the winged, torch-bearing, Eros-like Spirit of Earth easily lends himself to an identification with the traditional angelic guides of the spheres. Simply by drawing out and elaborating interrelations already latent in the given myths, Shelley has shaped a coherent and proportioned structure that embodies the interdependence of the One Mind and life-giving Love, and the bond between that all-embracing Love and the love that guides and is the joyous animating spirit of the earth: "L'Amor che move il sole e l'altre stelle."

This kind of tacit adaptation and restructuring of myths—nonreferential in that their meaning and value are not dependent upon or complicated by their previous forms of existence—is also at work in Earth's description of the cave to which Prometheus and Asia are forever to retire after their reunion (III. iii. 124–75). Beside this cave, says Earth, is a temple that once bore the name of Prometheus, where

> the emulous youths
> Bore to thy [Prometheus'] honour thro' the divine gloom
> The lamp which was thine emblem.

The controlling reference, E. B. Hungerford has pointed out, is to the lampadephoria, the torch race in which youths ran from the altar of Prometheus in the Academy to the Acropolis in Athens, the victory going to the first to arrive with his torch unextinguished.[24] The rather obvious possibility of likening this torch race to the

---

[24] Pausanias, i. 30. Sophocles' mention of a brazen threshold into the underworld near the altar of Prometheus in the Academy near Colonus

course of life had already been exploited by Thomas Taylor, who identified the burning lamp, emblem of Prometheus the Fire-Bearer, with the rational soul and added:

> This custom adopted by the Athenians, of running from the altar of Prometheus to the city with burning lamps, in which he alone was victorious whose lamp remained unextinguished in the race, was intended to signify that he is the true conqueror in the race of life, whose rational part is not extinguished, or, in other words, does not become dormant in the career.[25]

By rejecting the historical fact that the race was a relay, Shelley makes the symbolism entirely his own: the emulous racers are

> even as those
> Who bear the untransmitted torch of hope
> Into the grave, across the night of life,
> As thou [Prometheus] hast borne it most triumphantly
> To this far goal of Time.   (III. iii. 170–74)

The entire account of the cave and the journey to it, however, is in fact a conflation of many myths and symbols; for if the Promethean racers are like those mortals who, unassisted, carry hope through life to the grave, the "far goal" of their mortal time, and if both are like Prometheus the Torch-Bearer,[26] who has borne hope to that timeless perfection toward which all time moves, then

---

(*Oedipus at Colonus* 54–58) may have some bearing on Shelley's location of Prometheus' cave near his temple, as Hungerford suggests (*Shores of Darkness* [Cleveland, 1963], pp. 197–98).

[25] Pausanias, *The Description of Greece,* trans. Thomas Taylor (London, 1824), III, 224–25. Shelley ordered Taylor's translation shortly after its original publication in 1817 (letters to Ollier, 24 July and 3 Aug. 1817).

[26] Just as the shell is Venus' traditional emblem, the torch, as Shelley says and as the title of Aeschylus' lost play makes clear, was the emblem of Prometheus, who had stolen fire from the gods and given it to man. See, e.g., Euripides' *The Phoenician Maidens* 1121–22, where Prometheus is described as holding a torch; and Philostratus *Lives of the Sophists* xx: "Prometheus, torch-bearer and fire-carrier."

all are also like the Spirit of Earth, the Eros-like "torch-bearer" whose mother is the "Lamp of Earth," whose own lamp is kindled with love, and who has just been commanded by Earth to run ahead like the torch-racers and guide the Promethean company to the temple and the cave.

In addition, Earth describes the cave near Prometheus' temple in terms that associate it with yet another place. In the destined cave, Earth tells Prometheus,

>   my spirit
> Was panted forth in anguish whilst thy pain
> Made my heart mad, and those who did inhale it
> Became mad too, and built a temple there,
> And spoke, and were oracular, and lured
> The erring nations round to mutual war,
> And faithless faith, such as Jove kept with thee;
> Which breath now rises, as amongst tall weeds
> A violet's exhalation, and it fills
> With a serener light and crimson air
> Intense, yet soft, the rocks and woods around;
>
> . . . .
>
>   . . . and it circles round,
> Like the soft waving wings of noonday dreams,
> Inspiring calm and happy thoughts, like mine,
> Now thou art thus restored. This cave is thine.
>
>   (III. iii. 124–47)

Earth's spirit therefore was first panted forth in a place that tradition specified as the cave at Delphi, for legend tells that the first Delphic oracle was the infernal deity Gaia, or Earth; and Shelley's history of Prometheus' cavern is identical with the legendary history of the Delphic cavern. According to Diodorus Siculus (xvi. 26), the shepherds who first stumbled upon the cave were overcome by the volcanic vapors, fell into prophetic frenzy, and hurled themselves madly into the crater. How this destructive inspiration bears upon Shelley's ethical doctrine must be explored later, but obviously he has related it to the condition prevailing during Prometheus' captivity, the state of the "external" world being relative to that of the Mind whereby it exists. The Delphic prophetess who succeeded Gaia, many classical authors reported, was Themis, goddess of justice, or social harmony and peace,[27] so that it is quite proper that with the restoration of Prometheus the crimson vapor of the volcanic cavern inspire "calm and happy thoughts." Further, while some classical authors identified Themis as the daughter of Gaia, others, including Aeschylus, considered her the same as Earth; [28] and consequently Shelley does not at all distort the basic form of the myth when he describes the history of the cave as two successive stages of Earth's spiritual history. The same legend of the discovery of the Delphic cave also determines Panthea's picture of Demogorgon's oracular-volcanic cave, and it not only does so to analogous symbolic ends but also establishes thereby an important thematic rela-

---

[27] E.g., Aeschylus *Eumenides* 1–3. Abbé Banier claimed that "Themis is accounted only an allegorical Personage whose Name in the Hebrew Language imports *perfect* or *upright* . . ." (*The Mythology and Fables of the Ancients* [London, 1739], I, 290).

[28] *Prometheus Bound* 211–13: ". . . Themis, or Gaia (she has one form but many names) had foretold to me the way in which the future was fated to pass. . . ."

In his translation of *Prometheus Bound* Robert Potter wrote of Themis, "As she was the second prophetic power that held her oracular seat at Delphos, she was honoured as the goddess of Truth and Justice"; and in his note to lines 211–13 (quoted above), he added, ". . . Themis could not with propriety be called Gaia, this our poet mistook for Rhea. Gaia is the earth in its primitive uncultivated state, terra inculta; Rhea is the earth in its improved state of cultivation, tellus culta: and as from this culture property arose, Justice had here her office, to assign and protect this property, suum cuique: Themis therefore, as the goddess of Justice, might well have the appelation of Rhea" (*The Tragedies of Aeschylus* [2d ed.; London, 1779], I, 9n, 23n). The two stages Potter describes correspond closely to the two stages of Earth's oracle in Shelley's account.

tionship between it and Prometheus' cave. The portal to Demogorgon's cave is

> Like a volcano's meteor-breathing chasm,
> Whence the oracular vapour is hurled up
> Which lonely men drink wandering in their youth,
> And call truth, virtue, love, genius, or joy,
> That maddening wine of life. . . .   (II. iii. 3–7)

The self-destructive frenzy of the shepherds who first inhaled the volcanic vapors of the prophetic Delphic cave is not only the mad "mutual war" of earlier, uncivilized mankind when Prometheus was enchained; it is also the chaotic revolutionary frenzy of every man when in his deluding enthusiastic youth he first experiences the oracular truth.

But throughout, the Delphic cave and its legendary history, like the traditional accounts of the Promethean torch race, have been completely assimilated into Shelley's poem. To say that the story of the Delphic oracle is present in the poem either immediately or by allusion would therefore be rather more than the truth. In some hypothetical pre-text, we may say, torch-bearing Eros, Prometheus the Torch-Bearer, the Promethean torch race, and the legendary history of the oracle have been interconnected into a harmonious whole by means of syntactical possibilities they truly possess and then have been divested of their specific particularities so that the whole may constitute an archetypal shape for a group of the poet's thoughts. What may be said to exist truly is the beautiful potential order implicit in the connective possibilities among Eros, Prometheus, oracle, and torch race; and Shelley's lines are to be understood as an effort to embody that archetypal order, while the traditional ancient myths and rituals are but disarrayed and distorted fragments of it, or arrangements less nearly perfect than they might be. Shelley's narrative and symbols presuppose, and are sustained by, the archetypal form, and their existence is not dependent upon reference to any of its preserved embodiments.

III

But although Shelley's drama is to be thought of, ideally, as self-sufficient and independent of the heritage of the myths it has transformed and absorbed, and as being autonomous as a consequence of having totally assimilated those myths, nevertheless the poem also directs the reader to be conscious of the irony resulting from the clash between certain inherited materials and Shelley's transformations of them. In other words, I am suggesting that for a total reading the poem demands two contradictory states of mind at the same time. At one level the reader is to accept the various formulations in the play as nonreferential embodiments of archetypal arrangements and combinations, as though only Shelley's myth exists; at the other, conscious of the whole history of the myths, he is to experience the irony directed against the erroneous, evil, partial, imperfect, and distorted orderings that Shelley is reforming. The first level applies to the poem as an autonomous product, a self-sustaining myth in its own right, a "thought containing the principle of its own integrity"; the second, to the poem as a process, a calculated maneuver on the part of the poet to rectify the errors and imperfections of the past.

To this second level the reader is directed by the play's epigraph, which is, I believe, the only contradiction to the assertion that basic meanings in the drama are not dependent upon external contexts; or rather, it does not contradict the assertion because it stands before the drama proper, as though it were an instruction in how the play, at one level, is to be experienced. When Shelley recorded in his notebook [29] the line he adopted as his epigraph, "Audisne haec, Amphiarae, sub terram abdite?" ("Do you hear this, Amphiaraus, hidden away under the earth?"), he entitled it, "To the Ghost of Aeschylus," and the notation makes unquestionable the way in which it was to be applied to the drama. The line is one of the few known fragments of Aeschylus' *Epigoni*, and therefore it is with considerable irony that Shelley has turned it back on its own author. But since the words, as Shelley knew,[30] have been preserved only by Cicero in an anecdote concerning some Stoics, it becomes important also to be aware of its Ciceronian context. Cicero's disputation is on the subject of suffering pain and argues for self-mastery, the domination of the lower faculties by the higher, and the enduring of pain for the sake of reason and virtue. Pain is of such trifling importance that it is eclipsed by virtue so completely as to be nowhere visible.[31] After quoting from Aeschylus' lost *Prometheus Unbound* to illustrate the suffering of pain as it was endured by Prometheus, Cicero then tells the story of Dionysius of Heraclea, who, having been taught by the Stoic master Zeno that pain is not an evil, rejected the doctrine when he found he could no longer endure physical suffering. Thereupon, Cicero records, Dionysius' fellow Stoic, Cleanthes, lamenting the moral failure, stamped upon the ground and addressed the

[29] Bodleian MS Shelley adds. e.11, fol. 115.
[30] In his notebook, beneath the quotation, Shelley records, "Epigon. Aesch. ad Cic[?]." The reference is to *Tusculan Disputations* ii. 60.
[31] *Tusculan Disputations* ii. 66.

dead Zeno by reciting Aeschylus' question: "Do you hear this, Amphiaraus, hidden away under the earth?" In the history of philosophy, moreover, Dionysius became notorious for embracing Epicureanism upon his apostasy from Stoicism and was known contemptuously as the "Turn-Coat," or "Renegade" (Μεταθέμενος).[32] By using the line as his epigraph, Shelley, a latter-day Cleanthes, is similarly lamenting that the stoically resisting Prometheus of Aeschylus' *Prometheus Bound* was to become, in his terms, the weak, hedonistic apostate of the lost sequel who could not tolerate pain for the sake of his principles and submitted at last to tyrannical Jupiter.[33] But at the same time the epigraph addresses to Aeschylus, who had allowed his Prometheus to recant, Shelley's entire reorganization of the myth, in which the Titan will destroy tyranny by never weakening. The complex readdress of Aeschylus' line to its own author announces the ironic interplay that will take place between Shelley's drama and Aeschylus', so that while Shelley's is self-sustaining and independent of Aeschylus' for its form and significance as a work of art, it nevertheless calls upon the reader to contemplate what is being repudiated by the ironic workings of art.

The general ironic relationship between the two plays is too obvious and Shelley's "borrowings" have been elaborated too frequently to justify repetition here.[34]

---

[32] E.g., Diogenes Laertius *Lives of Eminent Philosophers* vii. 166–67.

[33] Preface to *Prometheus Unbound:* ". . . I was averse from a catastrophe so feeble as that of reconciling the Champion with the Oppressor of mankind. The moral interest of the fable, which is so powerfully sustained by the sufferings and endurance of Prometheus, would be annihilated if we could conceive of him as unsaying his high language and quailing before his successful and perfidious adversary."

[34] See, among others, *Prometheus Unbound,* ed. Vida D. Scudder (Boston, 1909), pp. 121–42; and Shelley, *Poems Published in 1820,* ed. A. M. D. Hughes (2d ed.; Oxford, 1957), pp. 191–215.

Broadly, his procedure is to draw heavily on Aeschylus' play but to reassign the "borrowings" and re-establish them in a contrary ethical and theological context so as to transform their meanings radically. Shelley retained as part of the machinery of his drama remarkably many of Aeschylus' details, such as the temptation of Prometheus by Mercury, Prometheus' invocation of the elements, and the catastrophic effects wrought on the natural world by Prometheus' defiance, to say nothing of a host of minor details and phrases. But whereas Aeschylus' play deals with the original binding of Prometheus, Shelley adapted all these events to a much later moment in time so as to apply them to Prometheus' eventual unbinding. That is, although his play appears to be the sequel to Aeschylus' *Prometheus Bound,* by recasting a great many of Aeschylus' details and speeches he implies that had the Greek dramatist not misshapen his myth and hence enslaved Prometheus, he could have cast the very same materials into their true unifying form and thus liberated and restored the Titan. In this sense, Shelley has not so much written a counter-myth as allowed Aeschylus' version of the myth to destroy itself, in accordance with his customary hypothesis that error and ugliness, if not willfully sustained, are self-defeating. As an example of this Actaeon-like technique of turning a myth upon itself we may take Apollo's report of Jupiter's fall, which he likens to the destruction of an eagle. Although traditionally supposed to be remarkable for its ability to gaze "on the undazzling sun," the metaphoric eagle has now been "blinded / By the white lightning" and plummets from the sky (III. ii. 11–17). But the eagle, of course, is the bird of Jupiter and serves here, by way of the metonymy wryly masquerading as a simile, as the god's surrogate. The lightning with which it is blinded is Jupiter's traditional weapon, and yet not only was the eagle the bearer and minister of Jupiter's lightning in the established myth but the tradition of unnatural natural history taught that the eagle was therefore impervious to its blinding light and could not be harmed by it.[35] Shelley has not merely denied the legend of the eagle; he causes it to contradict itself because Jupiter, like all forms of evil, error, and ugliness, wields a power which is only mistakenly thought to be a fearsome weapon against others and is fundamentally suicidal. This reflexive kind of irony is the central mode of representing evil throughout the drama, and correspondingly the irony of turning the line from Aeschylus' *Epigoni* back on its own author is of a piece with that of asking Aeschylus to hear the play he might have made of his materials had he known the true, the good, and the beautiful. Mainly by such a series of inversions, Shelley has created the beautiful harmony that is potential in Aeschylus' materials, rather than invented the sequel.

Aeschylus' Zeus is admittedly arbitrary and tyrannical, but we are told that he is new to his reign and can be expected to soften (49–51, 189–95); Shelley seizes only on the admission of tyranny, and his philosophy can allow the "immedicable plague" no mitigation. According to Aeschylus' theology only Zeus, within the limitations of Necessity, can possess complete freedom (49–50); but for Shelley only mind can be free, and to grant freedom to Zeus would be precisely the means of instituting absolute tyranny (I. 273–74, II. iv. 45–49). For Aeschylus, Prometheus' sin was not only defiance of Zeus's sovereignty but also an excessive love of mankind that led him to transfer to them powers beyond their due (122–23,

---

[35] E.g., Pliny *Natural History* ii. 55, x. 3; Apuleius *Florides* ii; Horace *Carm.* iv. 4. 1; Ovid *Fasti* v. 732.

29–30); for Shelley, of course, all power in this sense lies in the human spirit, which is where he locates divinity, and man's essential sin is to relinquish any of it. Shelley would have as man's due all that Aeschylus would assign to the anthropomorphic deity. And for Aeschylus' arbitrary foredooming Necessity, which is superior to Zeus and is determined by the Fates and Furies (514–18), Shelley has substituted the inherent Necessity whereby an effect follows regularly from a given cause.

Consequently, when segments of Aeschylus' play are specifically repeated in this quite contradictory context, blasphemy and righteousness often exchange places, and Shelley's text mocks the Aeschylean errors from which it derives. Occasionally it is sufficient for Shelley to display as true and good what Aeschylus offers as error and pride, such as Prometheus' defiant denunciation of Zeus for requiting him with imprisonment for his aid in the Titanomachy: "Such profit did the tyrant of heaven have of me and with such foul return as this did he make requital; for it is a disease that somehow inheres in tyranny to have no faith in friends." [36] Shelley sometimes modifies or alters an appropriated passage or detail,[37] for obviously he must reject such a speech as Prometheus' answer to the Chorus' question, "Is there no end assigned thee of thine ordeal?": "Nay, none save when it seemeth good to Zeus." Although Aeschylus provides that even if Zeus does not soften and release Prometheus, the Titan is foredoomed by the decrees of Necessity, Shelley cannot leave any room for the efficacy of Zeus's tyrannical capri-

[36] 223–27. Compare *Prometheus Unbound*, I. 380–94 and II. iv. 47–48.
[37] For example, by assigning to Aeschylus' cruel Hermes the beneficent character with which Aeschylus had endowed Hephaestus, Shelley has transformed him into the sympathetic Mercury who carries out Jupiter's revenge reluctantly and hates himself for his weak subservience, since Shelley's thesis is that slavery and self-contempt, or failure to value the powers of one's self, are causally related (see I. 352–60).

ciousness and allows only the inherent law of Necessity. To the analogous question, "Thou knowest not the period of Jove's power?" his Prometheus therefore replies: "I know but this, that it must come" (I. 413). On still other occasions Shelley can effect an irony simply by reassigning an Aeschylean passage so that the relocation helps shape what he holds to be the truest and most beautiful arrangement of which the materials are capable. For example, Hephaestus explains to Aeschylus' Prometheus that each relief from pain will be but another torment, in an endless cycle: "scorched by the sun's bright beams, thou shalt lose the fair bloom of thy flesh. And glad shalt thou be when spangled-robed night shall veil his brightness and when the sun shall scatter again the rime of morn. Evermore the burthen of thy present ill shall wear thee out; for thy deliverer is not yet born" (23–27). Shelley reassigns this speech to Prometheus, so that what in Aeschylus is a threat to the Titan of endless pain becomes the Titan's own triumphant stoic defiance of pain through faith in the inevitable workings of Necessity:

> And yet to me welcome is day and night,
> Whether one breaks the hoar frost of the morn,
> Or starry, dim, and slow, the other climbs
> The leaden-coloured east; for then they lead
> The wingless, crawling hours, one among whom
> —As some dark Priest hales the reluctant victim—
> Shall drag thee, cruel King, to kiss the blood
> From these pale feet, which then might trample thee
> If they disdained not such a prostrate slave.
>
> (I. 44–52)

One crucial and radical transformation, however, calls for special examination. According to the conventional myth, Prometheus ultimately revealed to Jupiter the secret that his marriage to Thetis would produce a son who would surpass and overthrow his father, and thereby he both prevented the marriage and bought his own release. By sacrificing his secret knowledge of the contingent decree of Fate, Prometheus humbled himself to Jupiter and assured Jupiter's supremacy. This sequence of events, so abhorrent to Shelley because it represented that voluntary enslavement which he considered both the cause and guarantee of all-powerful tyranny, he undermined by means of a complex system of inversions that at every point radically reconstitute the myth without ever abandoning its traditional elements or interpolating others. Shelley's Prometheus also possesses a secret known "to none else of living things, / Which may transfer the sceptre of wide Heaven" (I. 372–73), a secret that Mercury urges him in vain to clothe in words and offer up in submission to Jupiter; and in Act III Jupiter, wedded to Thetis, awaits the incarnation of their offspring. But it is significant that in Shelley's play the substance of the secret is never specified, nor is it ever related to Jupiter's marriage to Thetis, even though the absence of any other dependence of the play on Aeschylus' for basic meanings would seem to require that the secret be defined explicitly. Certainly there is no other ellipsis in the play that must be filled in by reference to Aeschylus. The secret of Shelley's Prometheus, then, cannot be the traditional one. If it were, certainly he could not be ignorant of "the period of Jove's power"; it would come whenever Jupiter's offspring deprives him of his throne, since Shelley's Prometheus, unlike Aeschylus', does not intend to divulge the secret to Jupiter. More important, the traditional secret, even though Prometheus were never to reveal it, implies that Jupiter could have been responsible for his own destruc-

tion or preservation by either marrying or eschewing
Thetis, and this would deny that the moral burden is entirely Prometheus', to say nothing of the triviality of rest-
ing the duration of Jupiter's tyranny upon his union with
Thetis. Shelley must place the moral burden entirely on
Prometheus, and hence the "secret" has no specific content. Prometheus' refusal is not the cause, even indirectly, of Jupiter's marriage, but is the general symbol of
his refusal to abdicate his will to Jupiter. For divulging
the mind's "secret" is, according to Shelley's symbolism,
essentially the act everyone performs in religious obei-
sance to a deity: "bend thy soul in prayer," Mercury
begs when pleading that Prometheus offer up his secret,

> And like a suppliant in some gorgeous fane,
> Let the will kneel within thy haughty heart:
> For benefits and meek submission tame
> The fiercest and the mightiest. (I. 377–80)

Prometheus has already constituted Jupiter by yielding
to him power over all things but himself and his will,
and, as Prometheus adds, what further submission remains but that "fatal word," the fateful "secret" which
symbolizes Prometheus' will (I. 396)? Jupiter is to fall,
not, as the Aeschylean myth would permit, simply because he produced an offspring mightier than himself,
but because Prometheus refuses that final abandonment
of power over his own will that would be implicit in
yielding up what is secret in him. Indeed, Shelley's play
in no way provides for the possibility that Jupiter could
have prevented his fall by avoiding Thetis; the causal
chain stretches back from Demogorgon to Asia and to
Prometheus' repenting of his curse and his refusal to
submit by revealing any "secret." What Shelley has retained of this portion of Aeschylus' myth, therefore, is

not the traditional explanation of the course of events; he has transformed that into a mere illusion entertained by Jupiter alone. Deprived of omnipotence by Prometheus' retention of his will, Jupiter is under the illusion that by marriage to Thetis he can propagate his own omnipotent perpetuity, only to find himself, in ironic fact, confronted by the force that will undo him.

In effect, the conventional myth not only is being readjusted to Shelley's philosophy but is being elaborately parodied. Fancying that his offspring and Thetis' has already been begotten and floats unbodied and unbeheld, "Waiting the incarnation" (III. i. 46), Jupiter expects it to be embodied when "the destined Hour" arrives (III. i. 20). It will bear, he claims,

> from Demogorgon's vacant throne
> The dreadful might of ever-living limbs
> Which clothed that awful spirit unbeheld
> (III. i. 21–23)

to trample out man's rebellious spirit. But of course Demogorgon's throne is not vacant—at least not in the sense that Demogorgon no longer exists—as Jupiter in his blinding pride believes. Nor is Demogorgon an embodied spirit. "I see a mighty darkness," says Panthea of Demogorgon,

> Filling the seat of power, and rays of gloom
> Dart round, as light from the meridian sun,
> Ungazed upon and shapeless; neither limb,
> Nor form, nor outline; yet we feel it is
> A living Spirit.   (II. iv. 2–7)

But Jupiter, whose very nature is distortion, cannot understand that Demogorgon is the unembodied eternal cause, the primal power infinitely remote from all that is

[88]

embodied, not a destructible being whose might is the "might of ever-living limbs." For religious and political tyranny, perverting every truth, imagines that power rests in the embodiment, the institution, not in that which is beyond all form because it is outside Being, or Mind, and absolutely different from it. In supposing that the unknowable Power can be incorporated in palpable human form, Jupiter not only has fallen into the ontological error of making power an attribute of being, but in fact is fabricating that anthropomorphism on which superstitious theologies are founded; or, as Shelley described the process in his notes to *Queen Mab,*

> It is probable that the word God was originally only an expression denoting the unknown cause of the known events which men perceive in the universe. By the vulgar mistake of a metaphor for a real being, of a word for a thing, it became a man, endowed with human qualities and governing the universe as an earthly monarch governs his kingdom.

There is, then, literally no "fatal child" at all; and the myth of Jupiter, Thetis, and their offspring is present only that it may be parodied in this manner, not because it is to be understood as the content of Prometheus' secret. While Jupiter falsely expects the ever-living limbs of Demogorgon to incarnate the evil that he himself is, ironically it is Demogorgon himself who appears, not to "trample out the spark" of man's spirit (III. i. 24) but to descend with Jupiter into inactive potentiality. Certainly Demogorgon, who is eternal, has not been begotten or caused by Jupiter in any sense; Jupiter's "child" is his misconception. Nor has Jupiter ever been responsible for stirring Demogorgon out of potentiality into action; this has been the effect of Asia as a consequence of Prometheus' retraction of his curse. Demogorgon, then, can say to Jupiter, "I am thy child, as thou wert Saturn's child; / Mightier than thee" (III. i. 54–55) only in the sense that each has displaced his predecessor and is greater in power; and the word "child" in this sense carries an immense weight of irony in view of Jupiter's expectations. The conventional myth, we are to understand, is quite as wrong in predicating that tyranny and falsehood could ever directly beget their own destruction as Shelley's Jupiter is in predicating that they could generate their own perpetuity.

Indeed, the union of Jupiter and Thetis is not, as Jupiter believes, a fertile mingling of "Two mighty spirits" productive of a third (III. i. 43); it is a sterile rape. In accordance with his methods of reforming the inherited myths, Shelley has called upon Jupiter's traditional character as rapist and has assigned to him the rape of Thetis that, according to the myth, was performed by Peleus after Jupiter had been forewarned.[38] As described by Shelley, Jupiter's rape of Thetis is to true union what tyranny is to equality and love; and because Jupiter is but the insubstantial, distorted reflection of Prometheus, it is presented as a gruesome parody of the love-union of Prometheus and Asia. Knowing that all hope is vain but love, Prometheus, in a passage that not only is implicitly sexual [39] but also has eucharistic overtones, had lamented his division from Asia,

[38] Ovid *Metamorphoses* xi. 229–65.
[39] In Bodleian MS Shelley adds. e.11, fol. 52, Shelley wrote, but not necessarily with reference to *Prometheus Unbound:* "In the human world one of the commonest expressions of love is sexual intercourse, & in describing the deepest effects of abstract love the author could not avoid the danger of exciting some ideas connected with this mode of expression, & he has exposed himself to the danger of awakening ludicrous or unauthorized images; but in obedience to an impulse. . . ." See also *A Discourse on the Manners of the Ancient Greeks Related to the Subject of Love.*

who, when my being overflowed,
Wert like a golden chalice to bright wine
Which else had sunk into the thirsty dust.

(I. 809–11)

With a brilliant insight into the mentality of tyrants, Shelley now has Jupiter describe to Thetis their "mingling" through "the desire which makes thee one with me," recalling with satisfaction that in the deed

thou didst cry, "Insufferable might!
"God! Spare me! I sustain not the quick flames,
"The penetrating presence; all my being,
"Like him whom the Numidian seps did thaw
"Into a dew with poison, is dissolved,
"Sinking thro' its foundations."

(III. i. 37–42)

Shelley, of course, has transferred to Thetis the fate met by Semele, who in return for Jupiter's embrace begged that he appear to her in the full splendor of his godhead and so was destroyed by his flames. "Her mortal body bore not the onrush of heavenly power, and by that gift of wedlock she was consumed." [40] Such, Shelley would have us understand, is the embrace of tyranny's power. Moreover, in echoing Lucan's description of Sabellus' physical dissolution by the seps's poison,[41] Thetis is crying out against the corruptive annihilation of her body by that supreme evil beneath which, if it were omnipotent, even the earth would vanish like thin mist (I. 115–16); and yet it is this that tyrannical power, knowing "nor faith, nor love, nor law" (II. iv. 47) and ignorant of the union of equals through love, conceives of as the act "which makes thee one with me" and gives birth to a third. It is by a further misconception that Jupiter

[40] Ovid *Metamorphoses* iii. 308–9.   [41] Lucan *Pharsalia* ix. 762–88.

thinks Thetis the "bright image of eternity" (III. i. 36) who will bear him the power that will make his tyranny everlasting; and hence the cutting irony that Demogorgon, who will unseat him, should now appear as his "child" and announce that among his various roles he is Eternity (III. i. 52)—not the endlessness of time, but the timelessness out of which time flows.[42]

IV

To adopt the Aeschylean myth in this fashion and yet to subvert it is, of course, to accept the ideal potentialities of the Prometheus story and yet to reject, by means of an irony, Aeschylus' formulation and interpretation of it. In other words, Shelley's conception of the difference between the potential Prometheus and the received myth is of a piece with his view of the difference between the life and doctrines of Christ and the Church's perversion of them for the purpose of fabricating an institutional religion presided over by a tyrannical and arbitrary deity. Consequently, just as the first three acts both echo and transform *Prometheus Bound,* one major stratum of the first act and some passages elsewhere derive in similar fashion from Scripture. Even apart from those moments when the life and figure of Christ enter into the main events of the first two acts, occasional muted adaptations of Scripture sporadically renew the slight quasi-Biblical tone. The horrors brought about by Prometheus' enchainment, for example, tend to suggest

[42] For Demogorgon as the timeless potentiality of time, see below, p. 216. In being described as the "image of eternity," Thetis is undoubtedly meant to represent endless duration. Note that Shelley first wrote "Shadow of eternity"; and compare II. iv. 33–34 ("Saturn, from whose throne / Time fell, an envious shadow") and *Timaeus* 37d.

the plagues visited upon the Egyptians for confining the Israelites in another kind of tyrannical bondage:

> Lightning and Inundation vexed the plains;
> Blue thistles bloomed in cities; foodless toads
> Within voluptuous chambers panting crawled: [43]
> When Plague had fallen on man, and beast, and worm,
> And Famine; and black blight on herb and tree.
>
> (I. 169–73)

Similarly, the miracle of Christ's walking on the waters, being one of those ideal orderings having "the power of attracting and assimilating to their own nature all other thoughts," can give perfect form to an expression of the spiritual effect of music:

> And music lifted up the listening spirit [44]
> Until it walked, exempt from mortal care,
> Godlike, o'er the clear billows of sweet sound,
>
> (II. iv. 77–79)

or to the ideal conclusion of Asia's backward journey over the symbolic waters from Age through Birth to a "diviner" region where "shapes . . . walk upon the sea, and chaunt melodiously!" (II. v. 108–10). On the other hand, a scriptural phrase wrenched out of context not only rejects Christian theology but, readapted to a wholly different context, constitutes a contrary vision. Hence Asia, upon describing the creative use man has made of Prometheus' gifts, asks,

> but who rains down
> Evil, the immedicable plague, . . . while
> Man looks on his creation like a God
> And sees that it is glorious . . . ?
>
> (II. iv. 100–2)

[43] Compare Exod. 8:3.
[44] On seeing Jesus "walking on the sea," the disciples thought him a "spirit" (Matt. 14:26).

For Shelley there is no supernatural Creator who looked on his creation and "saw that it was good"; in his homocentric theology only man's mind can be the source of the harmony and order that "create" the universe, the arts, and sciences. "All things exist," Shelley insisted, "as they are perceived—at least in relation to the percipient. 'The mind is its own place, and in itself can make a Heaven of Hell, a Hell of Heaven.' " [45] Nor is it the Christian God of the Apocalypse who dispels the first heaven and earth and sea to create a new heaven and a new earth.[46] In Shelley's concluding act this is exclusively the creative work of the powers of the human mind; indeed, while the Jehovah-like Jupiter existed, there could not be a heaven at all, so that the mind's powers must "build a new earth and sea, / And a heaven where yet heaven could never be" (IV. 164–65). And at this seemingly apocalyptic moment at the end of the play it is not God's angel who sets a seal upon the bottomless pit into which the serpent Satan has been cast and from which he will be loosed after a thousand years; [47] Shelley's serpent is not the supernatural power of evil, but the hieroglyphic serpent of temporal change, and its suppression is the work of the human powers of "Gentleness, Virtue, Wisdom, and Endurance,"

> the seals of that most firm assurance
> Which bars the pit over Destruction's strength;
> And if, with infirm hand, Eternity,
> Mother of many acts and hours, should free
> The serpent that would clasp her with his length;
> These are the spells by which to re-assume
> An empire o'er the disentangled doom.
>
> (IV. 562–69)

[45] *Defence of Poetry.* The MS reads "of itself," which probably represents the meaning he intended.
[46] Rev. 21:1.   [47] Rev. 20:1–3, 7.

[94]

But the primary function of the scriptural stratum of the play is that Shelley, building on the established tradition that made a Christ-figure of Prometheus, may draw out the identity of Prometheus' story and, as Shelley understood it, Christ's. Just as Prometheus has transmitted wisdom and power to a fictional Jupiter who, requiting good with evil, has turned these virtuous gifts against Prometheus and man, so, in Shelley's view, institutional Christianity has appropriated the virtuous life and doctrines of Christ and, by identifying them with a terrible and dictatorial God, has turned them into a despotism. Evil minds change good to their own nature and recompense virtuous gifts by enchaining the donor.

> The sublime human character of Jesus Christ was deformed by an imputed identification with a Power, who tempted, betrayed, and punished the innocent beings who were called into existence by His sole will; and for the period of a thousand years, the spirit of this most just, wise, and benevolent of men has been propitiated with myriads of hecatombs of those who approached the nearest to His innocence and wisdom, sacrificed under every aggravation of atrocity and variety of torture.[48]

"The wise, the mild, the lofty, and the just," Prometheus says to the image of Christ, "thy slaves hate for being like to thee" (I. 605–6); but the relation he is describing between Christ and enslaved Christians is also that between himself and Jupiter, who, when Prometheus cursed him, "trembled like a slave" (II. iv. 108). By identifying Christ with a hypothetically transcendent and punitive God, the Church transformed good into evil and became its slave, hating the good it had transformed; by accepting Prometheus' virtuous gifts of mental powers and transforming them into instruments of

[48] Note to *Hellas*, 1090–91.

vengeance and suppression, Jupiter has become their slave, hating both the virtuous Titan from whom he had received them and the race of mankind who are "like" the Titan. Both Jupiter and organized Christianity, the great tyrants, are slaves because "All spirits are enslaved which serve things evil" (II. iv. 110).

On the basis of these analogies Shelley's first act elaborately identifies Prometheus with Christ, and throughout the drama Christianity is repudiated by being ironically inverted, as Shelley has inverted the Prometheus myth of Aeschylus. The syncretic assimilation of Christ to Prometheus obliterates the specificity of the two myths to form the archetypal pattern, and although Christ is vividly recognizable by his description, nowhere is he specifically named, not only because "Thy name I will not speak, / It hath become a curse" (I. 603–4), but also because it would limit his reference. Prometheus absorbs Christ by a kind of inner requirement because both are manifestations of the same pattern of truth, and when he is forced by the Furies to look at the figure of Christ on the Cross he is really seeing himself. "Nailed" to the rock (I. 20) and pierced by the "spears" [49] of the glaciers (I. 31), Prometheus is obviously in the posture of the crucified Christ. Shelley's hero is the identity of both these pre-eminent types of superhuman and self-sacrificing resistance to evil, although it is part of the bitter irony of the inverted Christianity throughout the play that Shelley means the Jupiter who has crucified Prometheus to represent the God of whom the New Testament Christ is the incarnate son, and for whose redemption of man Christ endured the Crucifixion. Like the Christ he is, Prometheus "would fain / Be what it is my destiny to be, / The saviour and the strength of suffer-

[49] Compare John 19:34.

ing man" (I. 815–17)—but again with the crucial difference that he would save man, not from the sinful consequences of violating God's injunctions, but from the
mind-projected god who would tyrannize over man and
crush his independent spirit. For Shelley has formed
Jupiter with affinities with the jealous Old Testament
God of vengeance; and it is for the purpose of an inten-
tionally shocking repudiation of this God that Shelley has
reinterpreted the opening of Genesis to fashion Prometheus' malediction:

> Let thy malignant spirit move
> In darkness over those I love.[50]
>
> (I. 276–77)

The violent cosmic disorders that, according to Aeschylus, were wrought by Jupiter because of Prometheus'
defiance [51] and the corresponding disruptions of nature
that accompanied Christ's crucifixion easily lend themselves to Shelley's syncretic mythopoeia and its thematic
motive. As the Crucifixion was attended by earthquake
and the rending of rocks,[52] Prometheus' curse against his
tyrant-god and his crucifixion on the mountain, according
to Shelley, "made rock / The orbed world" (I. 68–69) and
brought tempest, earthquake, and volcanic eruptions (I.
166–68). The darkness at noon during the Crucifixion [53]
is represented by the "Darkness o'er the day like blood"
(I. 102) attending Prometheus' utterance of his curse. And
it is likely that the immediately preceding description of
the air's "still realm" torn by the curse and covered with
darkness when the rent closed (I. 100–3) parodies in
volcanic imagery the scriptural account of the conse-

---

[50] Gen. 1:2: "and darkness was upon the face of the deep. And the
Spirit of God moved upon the face of the waters."
[51] *Prometheus Bound* 992–96, 1014–19, 1043–50, 1080–90.
[52] Matt. 27:51.   [53] Matt. 27:45.

quences of Christ's giving up the ghost. For the irony lies in the fact that the received anagogical sense of the scriptural verse—"And, behold, the veil of the temple was rent in twain from the top to the bottom" [54]—is that by his sacrifice Christ opened a path into heaven. Mercury, sent by Jupiter to break Prometheus' will, is far less the threatening Hermes of Aeschylus than he is the Satan who tempted Christ by promising him all the kingdoms of the world "if thou wilt fall down and worship me." [55] For in return for bending "thy soul in prayer" to Jupiter, Mercury, unlike Aeschylus' Hermes, promises that Prometheus will "dwell among the Gods the while / Lapped in voluptuous joy" (I. 425–26); and whereas Christ refused because "it is written, Thou shalt worship the Lord thy God, and him only shalt thou serve," [56] this is precisely the authoritarian God under the name of Jupiter whom Prometheus rightly refuses to worship or serve. Christ rejected the joys of the world; Prometheus, the pleasures of a putative heaven because he would not be one of its "self-despising slaves" (I. 429). Such a heaven, Mercury admits, "seems hell" by comparison with Prometheus' self-esteem and self-mastery (I. 358).

In the light of this recurrent and, generally, ironic syncretism of Aeschylus' myth with that of the New Testament, we can now recognize that at the same time that Shelley, as we have seen, empties of meaning the myth of Jupiter, Thetis, and their offspring he also is mocking the Christian doctrine of the Incarnation. Not only has he, by elaborating the Jupiter myth, denied that tyranny, which mistakes rape for love and union, can beget its own perpetuity, but, by fusing with the tradi-

---

[54] Matt. 27:51. [55] Matt. 4:8–9. [56] Matt. 4:10.

tional myth Jupiter's expectation that his unbodied offspring will be incarnate in Demogorgon's (nonexistent)
limbs, he simultaneously ridicules Christianity's belief
that the godhead can be embodied (IV. 18–24, 42–46);
and no doubt Jupiter's announcement to his assembled
gods, "Even now have I begotten a strange wonder, /
That fatal child" (III. i. 18–19), parodies God's announcement to his assembled angels in *Paradise Lost*, "This day
I have begot whom I declare / My only Son" (V. 603–4;
cp. Ps. 2:7). To Shelley Christ is the highest form of
mind in the realm of being, not the personification of
Power; and therefore he is properly represented in
Prometheus. The error of Jupiter, the disfigured shadow
of Mind, is not only his belief that he himself is Power;
it is also Christianity's error of believing that its fictional
creation is Power and that this Power can ever be incarnate as the Son in the realm of being. In the context
of such a mesh of falsehoods, such a Son could only be
conceived of as "the terror of the earth" designed to
"trample out" man's soul, not as its savior (IV. 19, 24).

Unquestionably Panthea's dream-vision of Prometheus
liberated and revealing his perfection is an elaborate assimilation of Christ's Transfiguration, which made his
divinity manifest to the Apostles in a vision.[57] Just as
Christ's Transfiguration strengthened the three Apostles
in their faith and prefigured his future state of glory and
that of man after the Resurrection, so Prometheus' transfiguration, revealed to Panthea in a dream and, through
her, to Asia, both implants in the Oceanids the desired
goal that, by the law of Necessity, will draw them along
the causal sequence of their acts and foretells Prometheus' coming state of glory after Jupiter is removed and
the Titan is reunited with Asia:

---

[57] Matt. 17:9; or while they were "heavy with sleep" (Luke 9:32).

'tis He, arrayed
In the soft light of his own smiles, which spread
Like radiance from the cloud-surrounded moon.
Prometheus, it is thine! depart not yet!
Say not those smiles that we shall meet again
Within that bright pavilion which their beams
Shall build o'er the waste world?

(II. i. 120–26)

During the night upon a high mountain the Apostles saw that Jesus' "face did shine as the sun, and his raiment was white as the light," the brilliance being the effulgence of the inner glory concealed beneath his human form.[58] Correspondingly, an apostolic Panthea reports that on the mountain height the

pale wound-worn limbs
Fell from Prometheus, and the azure night
Grew radiant with the glory of that form
Which lives unchanged within . . . ,

(II. i. 62–65)

and the simile likening Jesus' brilliance to the shining of the sun dominates Panthea's further description of Prometheus: love

from his soft and flowing limbs,
And passion-parted lips, and keen, faint eyes,
Steamed forth like vaporous fire; an atmosphere
Which wrapt me in its all-dissolving power,
As the warm ether of the morning sun
Wraps ere it drinks some cloud of wandering dew
. . . .
And I was thus absorb'd, until it past,
And like the vapours when the sun sinks down,
Gathering again in drops upon the pines,

[58] Matt. 17:1–6; Mark 9:1–8; Luke 9:28–36; II Pet. 1: 16–18.

And tremulous as they, in the deep night
My being was condensed. . . .[59]

(II. i. 73–86)

One detail of the Transfiguration scene of the New Testament, however, is significantly altered to strip away
the theology and locate divinity in the One Mind, for
Shelley could not well incorporate in his creation the
bright cloud which "overshadowed" Christ in glory and
from which the voice of God said, "This is my beloved
Son, in whom I am well pleased." What Shelley is repudiating and what he is urging instead are made clear by
his substitution: the "overpowering light" of Prometheus' "immortal shape was shadowed o'er / By love"
(II. i. 71–72), an "atmosphere" that "Steamed forth like
vaporous fire" and was the effluence of his inner sun-
like glory. Shelley's deity is not the transcendent God of
the bright cloud, but the overshadowing love that rises
like a bright vapor from within Mind itself; and instead
of God's acclamation of His beloved Son, the apostle
Panthea hears Prometheus' voice calling on Asia, Generative Love.[60]

In the context of these transformations of the life of
Christ and their absorption into the career of Prometheus we can understand more richly the dramatic func-

---

[59] See also II. iv. 126–27: "Prometheus shall arise / Henceforth the sun
of this rejoicing world."

[60] II. i. 87–91. Later Asia's birth will also be described by Panthea in
terms of a similar transfiguration:

> love, like the atmosphere
> Of the sun's fire filling the living world,
> Burst from thee, and illumined earth and heaven.
>
> (II. v. 26–28)

Since she is to be understood as the condition of Prometheus' being,
when she is returned to her pristine nature during her night-journey of
reunion with Prometheus, she will again undergo the same transfiguration (II. v. 11–20).

tion of the Spirits of the Human Mind at the end of Act I. The act is precisely balanced by the torturing Furies and tempting Mercury on the one side and the consoling Spirits on the other, each acting on the soul of Prometheus. The Greek Furies, Jove's agents who traditionally torture and punish the evil, are here, through the characteristic inverting irony of Shelley's drama, powerless to crush the virtuous Prometheus. On the other side, the Spirits of the Human Mind have a Christian ancestry. Making their flights from the human mind to console Prometheus after his torments and temptations, they perform the work of the angels who similarly "came and ministered" unto Jesus after his temptation by Satan and who appeared to him "from heaven, strengthening him," at Gethsemane.[61] But if Shelley has made the Furies evil and impotent, he also rejected angels who descend from heaven: there is no transcendent deity who can arbitrarily choose to comfort the One Mind. Minds are their own spirits, their own divinity; and human minds, being the portions of the One Mind, are the only possible source of the powers that can console Prometheus, even though they must fall short of the power of Love.

The equation of Prometheus with Christ emerges to the surface of the drama in Act I in the chorus of Furies, who taunt Prometheus with a history of Christianity that is also Promethean. Removing a veil, the Furies reveal to Prometheus burning cities and the despairing ghost of Christ bewailing the havoc for which he has been innocently responsible. The "gentle" Christ who once smiled on the "sanguine earth"[62] is described and his history recounted in terms equally applicable to Prometheus,

[61] Matt. 4:11; Mark 1:13; Luke 22:43.
[62] According to Shelley, Christ sought to replace "the sanguinary Deity of the Jews" with "moral and humane" laws (*Letter to Lord Ellenborough*).

bestower of knowledge on man, so that what the Furies are presenting to Prometheus is in effect a mirror image of himself. The similarity of the two saviors is drawn out precisely: the knowledge the Titan gave man aroused a thirst that "outran" the waters of knowledge [63] and became the feverish thirst of "Hope, love, doubt, desire," which now consumes him (I. 542–45); Christ's words of "truth, peace, and pity" outlived him to become a poison that withered up these virtues, and the faith he kindled became a destructive conflagration until only the dim embers of faith remain and the virtuous survivors gather around them in dread (I. 546–59). Each virtuous gift became destructive of itself and those who received it. But of course this is the demonic version of the truth, designed to reduce Prometheus to despair, for obviously the hope, love, doubt, and desire generated by insatiable thirst for knowledge are good, not evil. The Furies deceptively conceal the fact that man has been crushed, not by the gift of knowledge, but by the tyrannic use of knowledge and power by an anthropomorphic fiction, Jehovah-Jupiter; not by the words of Christ, but by the conversion of them into the dogma of the Church. The purpose of the Furies in presenting the image of the crucified Christ to Prometheus is to persuade him of his futility because all who, like himself,

> do endure
> Deep wrongs for man, and scorn, and chains, but heap
> Thousandfold torment on themselves and him.
>
> (I. 594–96)

But Prometheus will immediately undo the Furies' falsehood by acknowledging that it is Christ's "slaves"—that is, those who serve the institution that has perverted

[63] Ecclesiasticus 24:29: "They that eat me [Wisdom] shall yet hunger, and they that drink me, shall yet thirst."

Christ's virtuous words into an evil, authoritarian Christianity—who hate the "wise, the mild, the lofty, and the just" precisely because these are Christ's virtuous disciples.

Moreover, by dramatizing the analogy between Christ and Prometheus, the Furies have so confused the two that they create a significant ambiguity exactly like the ambiguity in Act I that makes the Phantasm of Jupiter the mirror image of Prometheus when he uttered the curse. Having revealed the ghost of Christ despairing amidst the ruined cities of men, the Furies add,

> Past ages crowd on thee, but each one remembers,
> And the future is dark, and the present is spread
> Like a pillow of thorns for thy slumberless head.
> (I. 561–63)

The ambiguity of reference is calculated: ostensibly the words are addressed to Prometheus, but the details derive from the picture of Christ that the Furies have just painted. Christ and Prometheus are in fact one; the two myths coincide, and there is no distinction between Christ's "thorn-wounded brow" (I. 598) and Prometheus' head on a pillow of thorns. Indeed, when the Furies now look at Prometheus after having tormented him with this vision of the tortured Christ, what they see in him is Christ in agony, whose "sweat was as it were great drops of blood": [64]

> Drops of bloody agony flow
> From his white and quivering brow.
> (I. 564–65)

Appropriately, it is shortly after this echo of Christ's agony that the Spirits of the Human Mind will come to

[64] Luke 22:44.

comfort Prometheus, just as the angel strengthened
Christ at Gethsemane. But it is a shocking irony that,
with Prometheus brought to the height of his torture,
one of the Furies appropriate the words with which
Christ asked God's forgiveness of his crucifiers: "Father, forgive them; for they know not what they do."
Dispassionately the Fury thrusts at Prometheus what
would be the severest taunt of all if it were true, the necessary inadequacy of man's spiritual powers:

> The good want power, but to weep barren tears.
> The powerful goodness want: worse need for them.
> The wise want love; and those who love want wisdom;
> And all best things are thus confused to ill.
> Many are strong and rich, and would be just,
> But live among their suffering fellow-men
> As if none felt: they know not what they do.
>
> (I. 625–31)

For Shelley must deny the existence of the God whom
Christ invoked, the supernatural anthropomorphic deity
who may arbitrarily exercise forgiveness or, "having
called us out of non-existence, and after inflicting on us
the misery of the commission of error, should superadd
that of the punishment and the privations consequent
upon it." [65] Nor can Shelley accept either the present
inadequacy of man as inherent in his nature or his ignorance and other deficiencies as the objects of forgiveness. Instead, to Shelley the proper response is Prometheus': the Fury's account should torture because the
deficiencies are inexcusable; those not tortured by it have
resigned themselves to accepting the imperfections of
man's spiritual nature, and they are the ones to be pitied.
Christ's words, therefore, are not the grounds for super-

[65] Note to *Hellas*, 197.

natural pardon; they properly belong to the agents of evil, not to a redeemer.

Prometheus can recognize in Christ a mirror image of himself, not because there is some accidentally viable analogy between the two, but, we are to understand, because they are different expressions of a universal truth whose pattern is always the same: to promulgate virtue without the safeguard of love is to make that virtue available to tyranny, and tyranny will pervert that virtue into the means of evil despotism. This, then, is not only the history of Prometheus and Christ, as Shelley interprets them, but also that of the political state, the most immediate and burning example for Shelley being the French Revolution. Consequently, Shelley's syncretic mythopoeia provides that Prometheus, tortured with a vision of himself in Christ, also have a vision of a nation, presumably France, rebelling against slavery, only to see in horror that it then becomes the victim of a tyranny like that of Christianity and Jupiter. Shelley's myth identifies the legend of Prometheus with both political history and the course of dogmatic religion because the law that governs moral events is necessarily one and subsumes its manifest modes in state and church, the two institutions in which Shelley consistently located tyranny. Prometheus in agony, like the Christ whom he has looked on, is granted by the Furies what they tauntingly call "a little respite":

> See a disenchanted nation
> Springs like day from desolation;
> To truth its state is dedicate,
> And Freedom leads it forth, her mate;
> A legioned band of linked brothers
> Whom Love calls children—.
>
> (I. 567–72)

[106]

The nation's moral awakening parallels Prometheus'
arousing man from his vegetative, disenfranchised existence under Saturn by granting him wisdom, the birth-
right that had been denied (II. iv. 32–99). But another
Fury breaks in to deny that this band is Love's children:
" 'Tis another's." Because this accession to truth and
freedom has not been bred by love, but only by aspiration
to truth, freedom, and equality, tyranny usurps these
new powers as the evil instruments of a Reign of Terror,
just as Christianity and Jupiter did:

> See how kindred murder kin:
> 'Tis the vintage-time for death and sin:
> Blood, like new wine, bubbles within:
>   'Till Despair smothers
> The struggling world, which slaves and tyrants win.
> (I. 573–77)

Or, as Prometheus will reconstruct the same vision:

> Names are there, Nature's sacred watch-words, they
> Were borne aloft in bright emblazonry;
> The nations thronged around, and cried aloud,
> As with one voice, Truth, liberty, and love!
> Suddenly fierce confusion fell from heaven
> Among them: there was strife, deceit, and fear:
> Tyrants rushed in, and did divide the spoil.[66]
> (I. 648–54)

[66] Compare *A Philosophical View of Reform:* "From the dissolution of
the Roman Empire, that vast and successful scheme for the enslaving
[of] the most civilized portion of mankind, to the epoch of the present
year have succeeded a series of schemes on a smaller scale, operating to
the same effect. Names borrowed from the life and opinions of Jesus
Christ were employed as symbols of domination and imposture, and a
system of liberty and equality (for such was the system preached by
that great Reformer) was perverted to support oppression—not his
doctrines, for they are too simple and direct to be susceptible of such
perversion, but the mere names. Such was the origin of the Catholic
Church, which, together with the several dynasties then beginning to

Yet if we reconsider this process of myth-making it is evident that Christ and Christianity are not in fact named or explicitly identified in the drama. True, it is explicit that a figure on a crucifix is displayed to Prometheus; and yet when Panthea reports to Ione that she has seen "a youth / With patient looks nailed to a crucifix" (I. 584–85) it is impossible to say unequivocally that she has seen anyone other than Prometheus, who is every patient crucified savior of man. Nor indeed is the French Revolution ever specified, even though the Furies are attempting to reduce Prometheus to the kind of submissive hopelessness that beset those of Shelley's contemporaries who were disillusioned by its failure. The historical pattern Shelley has elaborated could equally well apply to his view of the history of Athens, Rome, Venice, or Padua.[67] In describing how contemporary Spain, for example, had moved from one tyranny into another, Shelley wrote that it has passed "through an ordeal severe in proportion to the wrongs and errors which it is kindled to erase"; [68] and this might serve as well as the history of the French Revolution to explicate Prometheus' vision. True, it was with respect to the French Revolution in particular that Shelley had said that "a nation of men who had been dupes and slaves for centuries were incapable of conducting themselves with the wisdom and tranquillity of freemen so soon as some of their fetters were partially loosened." [69] But his reference is unlimited when he writes:

----

consolidate themselves in Europe, means, being interpreted, a plan according to which the cunning and selfish few have employed the fears and hopes of the ignorant many to the establishment of their own power and the destruction of the real interest of all."
[67] See *Ode to Liberty* and *Lines Written among the Euganean Hills.*
[68] *A Philosophical View of Reform.*   [69] Preface to *Revolt of Islam.*

A Republic, however just in its principle and glorious in its object, would through violence and sudden change which must attend it, incur a great risk of being as rapid in its decline as in its growth. . . . A civil war, which might be engendered by the passions attending on this mode of reform, would confirm in the mass of the nation those military habits which have been already introduced by our tyrants, and with which liberty is incompatible. From the moment that a man is a soldier, he becomes a slave.[70]

Prometheus Unbound is cast in universal, not special terms, and is formed by Shelley's vision of the entire history of man's inevitable movement toward equality and freedom, from ancient Greece to the glorious future. His conception of history having been shaped by the recent sporadic eruption of revolutions for freedom throughout Europe and America, he conceived of the French Revolution as but an event in that progress, and he recognized the development that resulted in the Reign of Terror and the despotism of Napoleon as the type of all that prevents revolution from becoming freedom. Through Prometheus' vision of the mere rebellion against tyranny Shelley is observing that in all of history the release of the good in any of its forms, whether virtue, wisdom, or freedom, will, unless it is safeguarded by love, become perverted into a self-oppressive and therefore self-destructive force, just as Christianity has subverted Christ's doctrines and as Jupiter has subjugated Prometheus with Prometheus' own gifts. True revolution is rebellion governed by mutual love and benevolence; rebellion alone grows into self-destructive civil war that reinstates with its own gains what it was designed to overthrow:

[70] *A Philosophical View of Reform.*

If there had never been war, there could never have been tyranny in the world; tyrants take advantage of the mechanical organization of armies to establish and defend their encroachments. . . . A sentiment of confidence in brute force and in a contempt of death and danger is considered as the highest virtue, when in truth and however indispensable they are merely the means and the instruments, highly capable of being perverted to destroy the cause they were assumed to promote.[71]

However much the reader may be tempted to specify Shelley's references, the fact is that Shelley has consistently abstracted and syncretized archetypal patterns of religious and political history in the same manner that he has assimilated the forms or potential forms of various conventional myths by releasing them from their special particularities. Presented successively with archetypal visions of religious and political revolution, Prometheus has seen, by virtue of Shelley's myth-making processes, the two major expressions of his own inclusive archetypal history as the One Mind.

[71] *Ibid.*

CHAPTER III

⫷§ POWER, NECESSITY, AND LOVE §⫸

As NEARLY every critic of *Prometheus Unbound* has observed, the only dramatic struggles in the play take place in Act I, and all the subsequent action, including Demogorgon's almost effortless overthrow of Jupiter, proceeds without worthy opposition and hence without dramatic tension. Withdrawing the curse whereby evil subsists and resolving to endure pain rather than submit to evil are Prometheus' only moral decisions, the only assertions of his will. Thereafter he does not act, but is acted for and upon, and the course of events is determined by other agencies. Yet by retracting his curse of hate and stoically resisting all temptations to weakness, Prometheus exhausts all the capacities that Shelley assigns to the will; and the result of his utmost determinations is to make possible the unleashing of the revolutionary and reconstitutive forces that are external to him and that alone can advance the action in the subsequent acts. Were Prometheus a mortal man, one might legitimately protest against the absence of a sustained tension and against the protagonist's being relieved of all burdens after Act I while others carry out what would appear to

be his responsibilities. But the events of the first three acts
are not intended as a heroic human drama, and man plays
only an off-stage role. As Demogorgon's final words make
clear, Shelley never thought of earthly man, in contradis-
tinction to Prometheus, as ever to be released from the
strenuous moral resolution made necessary by the continuous threat of resurrected evil. The scope of the Promethean action is cosmic, not human; its end is apocalyptic, not utopian; and its agents are all the forces that
are, not merely the moral will.

Given the metaphysical level at which the play is
conducted, the possibility of a drama of continued moral
decision and a contest of antagonists is precluded by the
absence of a transcendent God who promulgates a moral
code and punishes or rewards and by the unreality of
Jupiter except as a mental contingency. Prometheus has
no antagonist but himself, even though once he has ob-
jectified his distorted self as Jupiter, he must be the un-
wavering "barrier" to the "else all-conquering foe." The
only real and autonomously existing actors in Shelley's
cosmic design are the One Mind and the indifferent
ultimate Power, together with its equally indifferent law
of Necessity. Shelley's optimism, therefore, is not founded
solely on mental capacities: perfection is the innate and
normal condition of the One Mind, not its creation. This
perfection will come about because mind permits it, not
because it struggles to build it, for the indwelling principle of Necessity drives to this natural end if mind will allow it to do so. Although evil, the unnatural chain of
events, is always potential, Shelley denies that it is an attribute of being and that the mind is limited to the formulation of moral codes designed to come to terms with
it. Evil is the "immedicable plague" that, once it infects,
must run its course (II. iv. 101); and the infection can-

not be doctored into a tolerable approximation of health because, like a cancer, "Evil minds / Change good to their own nature" (I. 380–81). It is, however, only immedicable, not irrevocable, just as Ruin, "Woundless though in heart or limb," nevertheless can be quelled (I. 787–88). On the other hand, Shelley will not admit that the effective revolutionary overthrow of evil and tyranny can be a violent, hate-filled destruction: violence begets only the means of further violence, in the same manner that the liberty released by the French Revolution became the "bewildered powers" of the next "Anarch," Napoleon.[1] The action of revenging evil is an evil; the passion of pity removes the ground on which it stands:

> For Justice, when triumphant, will weep down
> Pity, not punishment, on her own wrongs,
> Too much avenged by those who err.   (I. 403–5)

All the mind needs in order to participate in the ubiquitous natural force is a faith in its existence and the submission to it that faith implies—a faith "so mild, / So solemn, so serene" that any mind may be reconciled with this natural force by means of that mild faith alone.[2] The power—not to amend, nor even to destroy—but to "repeal / Large codes of fraud and woe"[3] is everywhere and always potential, ready to act whenever it is admitted by passive reception.

Act II, therefore, removes us from Prometheus in order to display the release of the repealing powers that are outside the One Mind. Correspondingly, the scene changes from the desolate, barren, and wintry setting of Prometheus' self-imposed suffering to Asia's luxuriant Indian vale at the very inception of spring, the season that belongs to Venus-Asia and symbolizes the dawn of

---

[1] *Ode to Liberty*, 175.   [2] *Mont Blanc*, 77–79.   [3] *Ibid.*, 80–81.

the new age. At this same moment Panthea joins Asia and recounts two prophetic dreams that had visited her the previous night while she still attended Prometheus and experienced the spiritual winter of his mountain peak. The first proves to be a prevision of Prometheus' transfiguration, a promise of the coming restoration of the One Mind to its unclouded brilliance; for the transfiguration, like that of Christ, is not an accession to glory, which "lives unchanged within" (II. i. 65), but a removal of the eclipsing evil that had hidden the inherent perfection. As a vision of the natural perfection of the One Mind, the subject of Panthea's dream is its spiritual condition, not the thoughts it generates and contains; and therefore it cannot be communicated by words, the function of which is to give palpable shape to thoughts, the measure of the universe. The subject is not being, but its ideal state. Even in her dream Panthea did not experience through her senses, but through an absorption of her soul: although Prometheus in glory commanded her to "lift thine eyes on me," she

> saw not, heard not, moved not, only felt
> His presence flow and mingle thro' my blood
> Till it became his life, and his grew mine,
> And I was thus absorb'd. . . .   (II. i. 79–82)

Capable of being experienced only by a spiritual communion, the perfection of being is beyond communicable thought, and "the rays / Of thought were slowly gathered" in Panthea's mind only after her release from her spiritual absorption (II. i. 86–87). For this reason Panthea's words describing the experience are to Asia "as the air," and Asia must "feel" the vision by commanding Panthea to "lift / Thine eyes" and (eyes being the windows of the soul) mystically seeing, beyond the "inmost

depth" within them, the "soul" of the transfigured Prometheus "written" on Panthea's spirit. Like Demogorgon's realm, the purity of being is imageless, although
the two differ in that the truths of Demogorgon's realm
are totally unavailable to mind, and the purity of the
One Mind, in the unity of which all images dissolve, can
be felt by a communion of the soul. The former is beneath imagery, the latter beyond it.

Panthea is unable to remember her other dream until
the first has been conveyed to Asia, and the implication
is that it can appear only in consequence of the first and
is dependent on it. Presumably, too, its subject is something other than the perfection of the One Mind, since it
is communicated by words; or, rather, it is conveyed by
a process that Shelley apparently meant to represent the
nature of all verbal communication. Because words, like
a Kantian category, give intelligible shape to thoughts,
Panthea's words fill Asia's "own forgotten sleep / With
shapes" that recall to Asia's mind thoughts analogous to
Panthea's and essentially the same in meaning (II. i.
142–43). Given the premise that nothing exists except as
it is perceived, presumably we experience words directly
only as themselves; as communicative signs they function by giving shape to thoughts and thereby arouse in
the auditor's mind similarly shaped thoughts already
resident there through prior experiences. Verbal compre-
hension is not merely mediate but also analogous. The
essential ontological difference between the two dreams
is contained in the fact that whereas in the first Asia
must directly experience something "beyond" the inmost
depth of Panthea's eyes (II. i. 119), Panthea's words describing the second succeed in restoring to Asia's mind
analogous episodes of a forgotten dream, in one of
which, commanding Panthea to look on her, she saw the

full meaning of the dream "in the depth" of Panthea's eyes (II. i. 161).

In contrast to the brilliant serenity of Panthea's first dream, the second is powerfully, nervously energetic, its "rude hair" roughening the "wind that lifts it" and its expression "wild and quick" (II. i. 127–29).[4] This energy is the essence of its meaning. The dream, which occurred to Panthea on Prometheus' wintry mountain, is a vision in late winter of a lightning-blasted almond tree that blossoms and then is deflowered by the frost wind, each leaf of the fallen blossoms bearing the command, "O, Follow, Follow!" The symbolism is not private, and at least from his reading of Pliny Shelley would have known that the almond tree is notable as the first of all those that bud in winter, blossoming in January and bearing fruit in March.[5] This impetuous and anticipatory characteristic of the almond tree had almost consistently been associated by the scriptural exegetes with Jeremiah 1: 11–12: "And I said, I see a rod of an almond tree. Then said the Lord unto me, Thou hast well seen: for I will hasten to perform it." For, as the exegetes explained the pun, the Hebrew word for "almond" is also the word for "hasten," and thus the "hastening" tree appears to Jeremiah in his vision as the sign of God's promise to fulfill speedily what is prophesied. The almond tree, therefore, had long been an emblem of anticipation, since it pre-enacts and prophesies in winter the coming events of spring.[6] Implicitly repudiating the divine providence that the symbol traditionally represented,

---

[4] In personifying the dream Shelley is adopting a practice common in Greco-Roman mythology. See also *Prometheus Unbound*, I. 726.

[5] *Natural History* xvi. 42.

[6] See, e.g., Filippo Picinelli, *Mundus symbolicus* (Coloniae, 1687), pp. 540–41; J. Masenius, *Speculum imaginum veritatis occultae* (Coloniae, 1664), p. 1012; Alciati, *Emblemata*, No. 208.

In Bodleian MS Shelley adds. e.12, fol. 36, Panthea's speech was to begin, "I had a dream of spring."

Shelley makes the image precisely appropriate to his conception of nature's processes as the ineluctable sequence of cause and effect fulfilling its own fixed requirements in all media; and the command on the petals, "O, Follow, Follow," calls on Panthea and Asia to submit to the course of Necessity and allow themselves to be driven by it. The budding almond tree is the proleptic winter sign of the regenerative spring in both the natural and moral worlds. Because it is symbolic of this irrepressible course of Necessity, the dream appears "wild and quick" in its compulsion to lead to the new order, and even the wound the almond branch has received from lightning cannot prevent its spring rebirth, any more than the moral regeneration can be suppressed by the evil inflicted on the mind by Jupiter, whose weapon the lightning is.

At first glance it seems curious that Shelley chose to symbolize the workings of Necessity in the natural world not by representing the overcoming of winter by spring, but by superimposing winter's destructiveness upon spring's new births and by heavily weighting the description on the side of the former rather than the latter. The winter wind blows down the blossoms of the symbol of nature's driving compulsion to rebirth, and the Necessitarian command is stamped by winter's hoarfrost on spring's "new-bladed grass, / Just piercing the dark earth" (II. i. 148–49). Even the comparison of the command on the fallen almond blossoms to the markings on the hyacinth which "tell Apollo's written grief" (II. i. 40) asks us to consider the grief of the sun-god of fertility when jealous Boreas, the north wind of winter,[7] slew his favorite youth, rather than the promise of the spring

---

[7] In some versions of the myth the wind-god is Zephyr, but the winter wind is obviously the one relevant to Shelley's context. For the substitution of Boreas for Zephyr, see Servius on Virgil (*Eclogues* iii. 62).

flower with which the god commemorated his loss. The full significance of this oddly biased emphasis must be postponed for the moment, and yet it is clearly implicit that although the almond blossoms have been blown down they will be succeeded by the fruit, that the new-bladed grass will grow despite the frost, and that the early spring hyacinth replaces Apollo's wintry loss. The vanishing winter, however blasting, is not the end of nature's life but the prelude to its renewal, and Panthea's symbolic dream of Necessity, like her flight from Prometheus' winter to Asia's spring, is a broad promise that since winter is passing spring cannot be far behind. The order of Panthea's two dreams, therefore, is itself a manifestation of the Necessitarian sequence: the prophetic vision of the transfigured Prometheus imaged as the brilliant sun must first be divulged in order to reveal, behind it, the dream of the powerful Necessity that drives to that perfect end.

II

It has long been obvious that the scene that follows, in which two Fauns comment on the passage of the two Oceanids through the forest, derives its materials from Virgil's sixth *Eclogue;* but the relevance of that *Eclogue* to Shelley's theme has not been considered. At least since Servius' commentary, the sixth *Eclogue* had been identified with Epicurean atomism, for it tells that Silenus sang to the Fauns of how,

> through the great void, were brought together the seeds of earth, and air, and sea, and streaming fire withal; how from these elements came all beginnings and even the young globe of the world grew into a mass.[8]

[8] 31–34.

That Virgil accepted the philosophy of Epicurus seemed fully confirmed by Donatus' account of Virgil's education in that philosophy and by many similarities in his poetry to Lucretius' poem. Whatever edition of Virgil, however ancient or recent, that the early nineteenth-century reader turned to, few would have failed to explain to him unequivocally the Epicureanism of the *Eclogue,* and most identified the two Fauns as Virgil and his friend Varo, and Silenus as their Epicurean tutor, Syro. Although the Epicurean philosophy, like Shelley's own, denies a divine external creator and governor of the world, it does not necessarily follow, it was generally thought, that Virgil also accepted the doctrine that the universe is directed by chance. The four basic texts in all traditional expositions of Virgil's thought are the Epicurean sixth *Eclogue;* the brief Epicurean passage in the second *Georgic* praising the man who, by knowing the natural causes of things, can dispel the fears of death and of a supposedly supernatural fate; the explanation in the fourth *Georgic* that the instinct of the bees is actually their participation in the infused divine mind; and Anchises' especially famous account in *Aeneid* vi of how the universe is maintained:

> Principio caelum ac terras camposque liquentis
> lucentemque globum lunae Titaniaque astra
> spiritus intus alit, totamque infusa per artus
> mens agitat molem et magno se corpore miscet.

> (First, the heaven and earth, and the watery plains, the shining orb of the moon and Titan's stars, a spirit within sustains, and mind, pervading its members, sways the whole mass and mingles with its mighty frame.) [9]

[9] 724–27. On these four passages alone, Jacob Brucker, for example, based his analysis of Virgil's Epicureanism in his standard history of philosophy, *Historia critica philosophiae* ([2d ed.; Lipsiae, 1766], II, 71–75). (Brucker's work was abridged and translated by William Enfield in 1791.) But almost any commentary on Virgil, such as Joseph Trapp's or John Martyn's, will center on exactly the same passages.

The two passages concerning the world-soul were customarily ascribed to the Stoic, Platonic, and Pythagorean doctrines of an *anima mundi,* and the discrepancies between those philosophies and Epicureanism frequently embarrassed Virgil's commentators, especially since Anchises also explains to Aeneas the transmigration of the souls. Sometimes it was proposed that Virgil graduated from one philosophy to the other, but the favorite way out of the difficulty was to reconcile the obvious differences by accommodating the doctrine of the world-soul to Virgil's basic Epicureanism. Edward Gibbon's interpretation of *Aeneid* vi can be taken as typical of those that would have come to Shelley's attention:

It is observable, that the three great poets of Rome [Virgil, Horace, and Lucretius] were all addicted to the Epicurean philosophy; a system, however, the least suited to a poet; since it banishes all the genial and active powers of nature, to substitute in their room a dreary void, blind atoms, and indolent gods. A description of the infernal shades was incompatible with the ideas of a philosopher whose disciples boasted, that he had rescued the captive world from the tyranny of religion, and the fear of a future state. These ideas Virgil was obliged to reject: but he does still more; he abandons not only the CHANCE of Epicurus, but even those gods, whom he so nobly employs in the rest of his poem, that he may offer to the reader's imagination a far more specious and splendid set of ideas [in the lines quoted above from *Aeneid* vi]. . . . The more we examine these lines, the more we shall feel the sublime poetry of them. But they have likewise an air of philosophy, and even of religion, which goes off on a nearer approach. The mind which is INFUSED into the several parts of matter, and which MINGLES ITSELF with the mighty mass, scarcely retains any property of a spiritual substance; and bears

too near an affinity to the principles, which the impious
Spinoza revived rather than invented.

I am not insensible, that we should be slow to suspect,
and still slower to condemn. The poverty of human language, and the obscurity of human ideas, make it difficult
to speak worthily of THE GREAT FIRST CAUSE. Our most
religious poets, in striving to express the presence and
energy of the Deity, in every part of the universe, deviate
unwarily into images, which are scarcely distinguished
from materialism. Thus our Ethic Poet:

> All are but parts of one stupendous whole,
> Whose body Nature is, and God the soul;

and several passages of Thomson require a like favour-
able construction. But these writers deserve that favour,
by the sublime manner in which they celebrate the great
Father of the Universe, and by those effusions of love and
gratitude, which are inconsistent with the materialist's
system. Virgil has no such claim to our indulgence. THE
MIND of the UNIVERSE is rather a metaphysical than a
theological being. His intellectual qualities are faintly
distinguished from the powers of matter, and his moral
attributes, the source of all religious worship, form no
part of Virgil's creed.[10]

Nonetheless, Gibbon insisted that Virgil is a "determined Epicurean," and, however dissatisfied he may
have been, he found in the poet the consistent acceptance of a pantheistic world governed by the infused
Mind and independent of any transcendent divinities.
Others even held that the doctrine of the world-soul is
really implicit in Epicureanism. The materialist La Mettrie, for example, was of the opinion that it is the hypothesis "de Virgile, et de tous les Epicuriens" that there

[10] "Critical Observations on the Design of the Sixth Book of the Aeneid"
(1770), in *Miscellaneous Works* (London, 1814), IV, 487–89.

is "une Ame généralement répandue par tout le corps"; [11] and of the *anima mundi* Cabanis wrote:

> Cette opinion fut celle des stoiciens: il paroît que Pytha-gore l'avoit enseignée avant eux; on pourroit même penser qu'elle n'étoit pas étrangère aux disciples d'Epicure, puisque Virgile ne fait pas difficulté de le prendre pour base du système général qu'il esquisse d'une manière si brillante, si riche et si majestueuse dans le sixième livre de l'Énéide.[12]

In sum, the recurrent practice of deducing Virgil's philosophy from a compound of the four texts—but especially from the sixth *Eclogue* and Anchises' speech in the sixth book of the *Aeneid*—had resulted in a picture of an Epicurean who, like Shelley, rejected the idea of a transcendent Creator and Presider to whom man and nature are subservient, and who substituted for Epicurus' chance an actuating and regulating world-soul. Shelley has obvious affinities with Epicurus, whom he called the most divine of philosophers [13] and whom Lucretius praised for liberating man from the tyranny of religion and the fear of death by attributing natural events to natural causes and making the threat of hell a mere superstition; [14] and with Virgil's infused spirit that sustains the universe Shelley could, with slight change, readily identify his own principle of Necessity, the immanent and self-fulfilling causal sequence that is neither a conscious guiding mind nor a teleological force, but the fixed law of the energy that effects the course of events. The relevance of Virgil's sixth *Eclogue*, therefore, is that

[11] *L'Homme machine,* ed. Aram Vartanian (Princeton, N.J., 1960), p. 188.
[12] Pierre Cabanis, *Oeuvres philosophiques,* ed. C. Lehec and J. Caze-neuve (Paris, 1956), II, 282.
[13] See Roy R. Male and J. A. Notopoulos, "Shelley's Copy of Diogenes Laertius," *RES,* LIV (1959), 20.
[14] *De rerum natura* i. 62–79.

it is a mythic form, already resident in the human mind, that gives shape to a thought approximating Shelley's atheism and immanent Necessitarianism; and the scene in which Shelley introduces the Fauns dramatizes the Necessity that is the subject of Panthea's second dream. Just as Virgil's Epicurean Silenus had taught his students, the Fauns, how the world was formed by forces in nature, so Shelley's young Fauns, similarly inquiring into the principles of nature, seek to know where these powers live that, by "Demogorgon's mighty law" of Necessity, draw "All spirits on that secret way" (II. ii. 43–45).

The setting of this scene is a dark forest through which Panthea and Asia are driven by some external compulsion and of which the Fauns, woodland deities, are natives. In these woods, they say, "We haunt within the least frequented caves / And closest coverts, and we know these wilds" (II. ii. 66–67). The peculiar character of this forest, which is the limited area of the Fauns's inquiry, is carefully defined, for there grow "cedar, pine, and yew, / And each dark tree that ever grew" (II. ii. 2–3); and this universality suggests that it is as inclusively the world as is the garden of *The Sensitive Plant,* where grow "all rare blossoms from every clime." Just as the referent of Shelley's universal garden is the universal Garden of Adonis, on which the setting of *The Sensitive Plant* is based, so his universal forest derives from the traditional interpretation of *silva.* As the commentaries on the *lucus* of *Aeneid* vi. 13 or the *silva* of vi. 131 recurrently pointed out, "silva materiam notat," for the Greek *hyle* means both wood and the basic matter of which the world is formed; or, as Shelley would have read in Thomas Taylor's *Dissertation on the Eleusinian and Bacchic Mysteries,* when Virgil in his sixth book "says that all the middle regions are covered with woods, this too plainly intimates a material nature; the word silva, as is well known, being used by ancient writers to signify matter, and implies nothing more than that the passage . . . is through the medium of a material nature."[15] In his *Epipsychidion* Shelley leaves no doubt that the "wintry forest" there represents the domain of mortal life (249–344), and, similarly, the forest of the Fauns is what man customarily designates as the world of matter.[16] Virgil's Epicurean Fauns have been appropriated to comment on the operation of the laws of Necessity in that realm.

Indeed, the "Spirits" about whom the Fauns inquire have already sung of how Necessity performs in both the natural and human worlds. One semichorus of the Spirits explains that when one nightingale in the dark woods, "Sick with sweet love," allows its song to die away, another "catches" the "languid close" to lift the song anew (II. ii. 31–32).[17] This instinctual urge that perpetuates the undulating decline and resurgence of the song,[18] like the instinct that Virgil's bees possess as their portion of the active spirit infused throughout all

[15] In *The Pamphleteer* (2d ed.; London, 1816), VIII, 42, 462. Taylor makes the same point in his notes on Proclus (*The Philosophical and Mathematical Commentaries* [London, 1792], II, 300–1n). This definition is, of course, the reason why Bacon entitled his study of natural history *Sylva sylvarum*. But, as Taylor points out, the information was in the common domain, and it was recorded, among other places, in nearly every Latin dictionary.

[16] In addition, the "gloom divine" of the forest (II. ii. 22) is clearly meant to represent the condition of mortal life: the "divine gloom" through which the Promethean racers run is explicitly equated with "the night of life" (III. iii. 169, 172), and the Spirits of Necessity sing of "the gloom to Earth given" (II. iii. 78).

[17] Shelley's terms, of course, derive from the catch-song and musical "close," or cadence. The word "bear" (II. ii. 34), meaning "sustain," also derives from its use as a musical term, as in the phrase "bear the burden."

[18] At one point in the draft of these lines Shelley wrote, "that aye renewed strain" (Bodleian MS Shelley adds. e.12, fol. 32).

[124]

things,[19] is, of course, the immanent working of Necessity. And just as Virgil drew an analogy between the instinctive acts of the bees and the actions of man, so Shelley's other semichorus replies by singing of Necessity in human actions. Like Panthea and Asia in their passage through the forest, the semichorus explains, men believe they are the arbitrary masters of their actions, but those who know the philosophic truth ("those who saw") are aware that it is "Demogorgon's mighty law" of Necessity that draws out of any cause its ineluctable chain of effects: the Oceanids are driven on a route that is "secret" (because Necessity, or the causative process, is not an empirical datum)

> As inland boats are driven to Ocean
> Down streams made strong with mountain-thaw:
> > And first there comes a gentle sound
> > To those in talk or slumber bound,
> > And wakes the destined—soft emotion
> Attracts, impels them: [20] those who saw
> > Say from the breathing earth behind
> > There steams a plume-uplifting wind [21]
> Which drives them on their path, while they
> > Believe their own swift wings and feet
> The sweet desires within obey.   (II. ii. 46–56)

As Asia awakens the slumbering Demogorgon to action in accordance with his inviolable law of process, and as Eternity must unloose the snakelike "Doom" of temporal sequence (II. iii. 95–97), so the sound awakens what is "destined" because Shelley's doctrine of causal Necessity

---

[19] *Georgics* iv. 219–24.

[20] I have adopted the reading of Shelley's MS fair copy instead of the unintelligible version in the 1820 text: "And wakes the destined soft emotion, / Attracts, impels them." I hope the interpretation that follows will justify the choice.

[21] I.e., a wind that uplifts the plumes of Asia's and Panthea's wings and so drives them on their path.

provides that an effect is not random but is implicit in its cause, a consequence in its motive. The "relation which motive bears to voluntary action is that of cause to effect"; and it is false to "assert that the will has the power of refusing to be determined by the strongest motive." [22] To arouse motive is to arouse the whole inevitable course of "voluntary" action that it destines; and "emotion," [23] or the principle of the relations among these successive actions, is manifest as the same attraction and repulsion ("Attracts, impels them") that is observed to govern motion in the sensible world. But the actual causative force of human action—the "plume-uplifting wind"—derives from an ultimate source infinitely remote from being: Power, the source of motion and emotion, is not an attribute of mind or of its faculty of will.

Having heard these Spirits sing of Necessity, one Faun then asks where they live, for, although the Fauns, like earthly man, are indigenous to the world of matter and inhabit its deepest recesses, they, too, have never met with their senses the causative Spirits. The second Faun's reply is an exemplary description of the way in which the invisible Necessity works in the physical world. He has heard the masters of natural philosophy— "those more skilled in spirits"—say that

> The bubbles, which the enchantment of the sun
> Sucks from the pale faint water-flowers that pave
> The oozy bottom of clear lakes and pools,
> Are the pavilions where such dwell and float
> Under the green and golden atmosphere
> Which noon-tide kindles thro' the woven leaves;

[22] Note to *Queen Mab* on "Necessity." Shelley repeated this doctrine in his *Speculations on Morals* and *On the Devil and Devils*.
[23] For the probable pun here on "emotion," see below, Chapter IV, n. 27.

And when these burst, and the thin fiery air,
The which they breathed within those lucent domes,
Ascend to flow like meteors thro' the night,
They ride on them, and rein their headlong speed,
And bow their burning crests, and glide in fire
Under the waters of the earth again.   (II. ii. 71–82)

This novel description of the cycle of the will-o'-the-wisp, no doubt Shelley's invention, is founded on the fact that gases, or "fiery air," were known to be exhaled from marshy ground and to "ignite" as "meteors"; and Shelley evidently held some idiosyncratic theory that this "wandering Meteor," as he described the will-o'-the-wisp in *The Revolt of Islam,* after rising "from the morass" and shining with a "wondrous light," then returns "to its far morass." [24] Perpetually alternating as bubbles in the water and meteoric lights in the atmosphere, the "fiery air," like the nightingales' song, represents all the cycles of nature's changes: the actuating "spirits" that dwell in the bubbles in the oozy bottom and then ride the meteors remain constant while the form that invests them undergoes a repeated sequence of alterations.[25] Like Virgil's Fauns, who were instructed in an atheistic cosmogony, Shelley's gain intimations of the presence in nature of the atheistic Necessitarianism that the chorus of Spirits had already represented in nature's processes and in human actions.

In Panthea's and Asia's dreams the commands to follow, we have noted, are somewhat ambiguous. Although the conjunction of winter's blight and spring's growth clearly must represent the rebirth of spring out of the dying winter, it is on the fallen, winter-blasted almond

[24] *Revolt of Islam,* VI. xxxii–xxxiv.
[25] Compare *Mont Blanc,* where Necessity transforms the snow on the peak into the murderous glaciers and then into the life-giving River Arve.

blossoms that the command is stamped, even though the tree itself is pre-eminently the prophecy of the coming spring. Although the order to follow appears on the new grass of spring, it was printed there by the hoarfrost and was revealed only when the frost had melted away: the melting frost, not the burgeoning grass, demands to be followed. "Follow, O Follow" was cast on the mountain slope by the clouds "as they vanished by" (II. i. 153). The music of the pine boughs calling, "O, Follow, Follow, Follow Me!" sounds like the "farewell of ghosts" (II. i. 157–59); and the Echoes who draw the Oceanids on their path are receding voices, like dew evaporating in the morning sun (II. i. 167–76). The hastening upsurge of the new year's life is contemporaneous with the vanishing of the old year's winter, but Asia and Panthea are being compelled to follow the old order of things as it shrinks out of existence, not the new birth. Winter, together with all that it symbolizes, is not destroyed; it is forced to recede from the palpable world into its impalpable origin in the same manner that the audible Echoes drawing the Oceanids are receding into the caves, their traditional native home, where they reside, inaudible.[26] Clearly "Demogorgon's mighty law" that draws Panthea and Asia is the Necessitarian law of fixed and inviolable sequences, for it draws them down to Demogorgon's realm

> As the fawn draws the hound,
> As the lightning the vapour,
> As a weak moth the taper;
> Death, despair; love, sorrow;

[26] See, e.g., Ovid *Metamorphoses* iii. 394.
   In one of his notebooks Shelley wrote, "The spring rebels not against winter but it succeeds it—the dawn rebels not against night but it disperses it" (Bodleian MS Shelley adds. e.18, flyleaf).

Time both; to-day, to-morrow;
As steel obeys the spirit of the stone,
                    Down, down.
                                        (II. iii. 65–71)

But it is compelling them to retreat from the sensible world, as the winter, the melting hoarfrost, the fading music, and the receding echoes are retreating, into the impalpable ultimate force behind the law of Necessity. For the old order must be withdrawn into its remote, inactive source in order that the new order may be released from its ultimate springhead into the sensible world.

To be drawn by the Spirits, Panthea and Asia are required not to act autonomously but to submit to Necessity by an act of will, or, as they think of it, to obey their "sweet desires." For if, as Shelley believes, evil is an unnatural distortion imposed by the will upon the good and true, it will vanish of itself if man willfully, as though by an act of faith, submits his will to the laws of nature. "Resist not the weakness" of passive submission to Necessity, the Oceanids are urged;

Such strength is in meekness
That the Eternal, the Immortal,
Must unloose through life's portal
The snake-like Doom coiled underneath his throne
                    By that alone.
                                        (II. iii. 93–98)

The significance of these words rests on the recognition that Demogorgon, "the Eternal, the Immortal," to whose realm Panthea and Asia are being drawn, represents Power as it was defined above in Chapter I. Shelley's atheistic idealism, we noted, drove him to divorce ultimate cause absolutely from the One Mind, or being. In the palpable world, where the cycle of the will-o'-the-wisp is the pattern of natural events,

> All things that move and breathe with toil and sound
> Are born and die; revolve, subside, and swell;

but the "Power," or ultimate source of this recurrent cycle, "dwells apart in its tranquillity, / Remote, serene, and inaccessible." This, Shelley writes in *Mont Blanc*, he had learned by tracing events to their beginning in time (the "primaeval"), only to learn that he was still short of their cause: the span between the first perceptible event in being and its ultimate cause is infinite. In that poem he had symbolized the unknowable Power as the inaccessibly transcendent and perpetual falling of the snow on the mountain peak—a totally indifferent Power that is beyond all sensible qualities because it is their absolute source. Itself eternal and immutable, it is the cause of all that is temporal and mutable in the world:

> Mont Blanc yet gleams on high:—the power is there,
> The still and solemn power of many sights,
> And many sounds, and much of life and death.
> In the calm darkness of the moonless nights,
> In the lone glare of day, the snows descend
> Upon that Mountain; none beholds them there,
> Nor when the flakes burn in the sinking sun,
> Or the star-beams dart through them:—Winds contend
> Silently there, and heap the snow with breath
> Rapid and strong, but silently! Its home
> The voiceless lightning in these solitudes
> Keeps innocently, and like vapour broods
> Over the snow. The secret Strength of things
> Which governs thought, and to the infinite dome
> Of Heaven is as a law, inhabits thee!   (127–41)

In *Prometheus Unbound* this "secret Strength" located outside "life's portal" is represented by Demogorgon; and that Power releases its normal processes into the realm of life when the mind bends its will into the passive admission of them.

Inasmuch as ultimate cause is infinitely remote from the first palpable event in the regular temporal chain called cause and effect, Demogorgon's realm is absolutely remote not only from the universe but also from the One Mind by which the universe is constituted; and it is notable that Prometheus and Demogorgon never meet, indeed could not. Even though Asia, as the generative love which is the ideal state of the One Mind, does enter Demogorgon's domain, she learns that there its truths are "imageless" and therefore are as unavailable to mind as is the imageless peak of Mont Blanc. Correspondingly, Demogorgon himself is imageless, being "Ungazed upon and shapeless" and having "neither limb, / Nor form, nor outline" (II. iv. 5–6). Since thought is the measure of the universe and since Power is distinct from that universe, Demogorgon's is "the world unknown" (II. i. 190). The distinction is not one between the One Mind, which constitutes the universe, or known world, and a yet greater Mind which constitutes the "world unknown." Shelley has not slipped into a Kantian distinction between phenomenal and noumenal worlds, nor is Demogorgon a God that Shelley has been tricked into admitting while elaborating an atheistic metaphysics. There is only the One Mind (and its human modes) and the one universe that exists by virtue of being the object of its thought. Demogorgon cannot be mind at all because

that the basis of all things cannot be, as the popular philosophy alleges, mind, is sufficiently evident. Mind . . . cannot create, it can only perceive. It is said also to be the cause. But cause is only a word expressing a certain state of the human mind with regard to the manner in which two thoughts are apprehended to be related to each other. . . . It is infinitely improbable that the cause of mind, that is, of existence, is similar to mind.[27]

Consequently Prometheus is represented anthropomorphically, but Demogorgon is not. Although a "living Spirit," he has none of the attributes of mind—neither will, nor thought, nor passion—and appears only as a "mighty darkness" (II. iv. 7, 2; IV. 510). Since Shelley has equated mind with "existence" and therefore has identified thought with the universe of being, at the point in his manuscript where he located Demogorgon's realm in "the world unknown," he contemplated adding, "Beyond the world of being." [28] The route to this realm in "the depth of the deep" (II. iii. 81) leads down through the sensible world of mortal life; through that point of entrance and exit where Death and Life strive with each other; beyond the barrier separating our mutable human world, where things "seem," from that realm where things "are"; down to "the remotest throne" (II. iii. 54–61), the infinitely distant ultimate Power, or Cause, the "One" whence the succession of sensible events flows (II. iii. 79). Demogorgon is not, as some have proposed, Necessity, the "mighty law" governing the regular events flowing from or receding to him; Necessity is Demogorgon's law and is immanent in Prometheus' reality, the "world of being," as Demogorgon is not. Nor is it adequate to interpret him as Destiny or Revolution, as other critics have proposed, although, like all other events, these are implicit in Power. In Shelley's words, he occupies "the seat of power" (II. iv. 3), and Mary Shelley was right to call him "the Primal Power of

[27] *On Life.*   [28] Bodleian MS Shelley adds. e.11, fol. 111.

the world," although we must also recognize his isolation and absolute difference from the world. He is, in brief, infinite potentiality, needing only to be roused in order to release his force into the realm of being as a chain of events. Otherwise dormant in his unknowable world, he is

> Like veiled lightning asleep,
> Like the spark nursed in embers,
> The last look Love remembers,
> Like a diamond, which shines
> On the dark wealth of mines.
>
> (II. iii. 83–87)

He is the "voice unspoken" (II. i. 190), the treasured "spell" (II. iii. 88)—the word that, on being spoken, has causal power.[29]

Since mind has no immediate access to Power, Prometheus cannot be the agent to rouse Demogorgon from his sleep; he has reached the outer limits of his reformative capacity when he withdraws the hate that has sustained Jupiter and willfully submits his will to the law of Necessity. Only Asia, generative love, serving as agency of the One Mind and acting under the compulsion of Necessity, can retreat into potentiality and awaken it. The removal of hate is only a negative act; it can only prepare the way for Love to activate Power. Asia's retreat from the world of being into the realm of the potential, then, motivates the parallel withdrawal of Jupiter by Power into its own potentiality, and thus makes possible

[29] An abandoned stanza in Huntington MS 2177, fol. 6ᵛ, further likens this potentiality to

> a dew mist asleep
> Which the winds might embolden
> To climb bright & golden
> Up to the vault of the dawn
> Till the sun rides thereon.

[133]

the release of the "natural" course of events, symbolized by Asia's flight from the realm of potentiality to active reunion with Prometheus.

III

With these interpretations in hand, we can now return to a consideration of the significance of Asia's route and, thus, the structure of Act II. We have observed that the two *loci classici* of Virgil's philosophy were understood to be the Silenus *Eclogue* and the sixth book of the *Aeneid* and that, taken together, these were generally read as forming a modified Epicureanism which denies a divine Creator and Governor and postulates an infused spirit that sustains and moves the world. Consequently, the sixth *Eclogue* was an appropriate significant form that Shelley could adapt to represent the operation of Necessity in a physicomoral world devoid of a God. Like Virgil's Fauns, who learn how the atoms came together of themselves to form the world, Shelley's Fauns have learned of the immanent Necessity which directs both the events of nature and the journey of Panthea and Asia through the forest of the sensible world. In the scene following this bucolic episode, the Oceanids then descend through a volcanic crater into Demogorgon's mysterious cave, and there Asia questions the ultimate cause about the ultimate truths.

In other words, this *descensus ad inferos* of the Oceanids is very like Aeneas' underworld journey in the sixth book of the *Aeneid*. Drawn to the mountain peak, Asia sees that "midway" below her it is "around / Encinctured by the dark and blooming forests" (II. iii. 24–25), just as the Sibyl had told Aeneas that between the upper

air and the underworld, "tenent media omnia silvae," [30]
or, as Dryden had amplified the sense, "Deep forests and
impenetrable night / Possess the middle space." Beneath
her is a cavern like "a volcano's meteor-breathing chasm,
/ Whence the oracular vapour is hurled up" (II. iii. 3–
4), the analogue of which is Virgil's gate to the underworld through a cave among volcanic mountains and
near the cave whose volcanic vapors inspired the Cu-
maean Sibyl. Thence the "Spirits" of Necessity, having
"bound" Asia and Panthea and assuming the role of Aeneas' Sibyl, "guide" them to Demogorgon (II. iii. 90). In
Scene 2 Panthea and Asia have experienced in the sensible world the omnipresent activity of Necessity, and now
they are to encounter, beneath the sensible world, the
Power from which the law of Necessity issues; and correspondingly the significant form provided by Virgil's
sixth *Eclogue*, which offers, directly or indirectly, an
antitheological explanation of the self-governed sensible
world, is replaced by that of the sixth book of the *Aeneid*, which offers an antitheological account of the
anima mundi, one of the secrets buried in the depths and
darkness beneath the earth.[31] The essential differences
between Shelley's adaptation and the received interpretation of Virgil are that the *anima mundi*, unlike Demogorgon, is a mind, an intelligence; and that it is Demogorgon's law of Necessity that, like the *anima mundi*, is
immanent in nature, not Demogorgon, who is outside it.

When Aeneas encounters his father, Anchises, in the
underworld, he gains from him revelations of two distinct
kinds: one explains the nature and actions of the world-
soul and of the human soul; the other prophesies the fu-

---

[30] *Aeneid* vi. 131. The glossators noted: "per silvas, tenebras et lustra
significat."
[31] *Ibid.*, 266–67.

ture glories of his royal line, glories that are to culminate in the return of the Golden Age in the reign of Augustus. As Dryden marked these two themes in his succinct "Argument" of the book, Anchises instructs Aeneas "in those sublime mysteries of the soul of the world, and the transmigrations; and shews him that glorious race of heroes which was to descend from him, and his posterity." Correspondingly, Asia's first questions of Demogorgon in the underworld have to do with the theology of creation: Who created the objective "living world"? Who created the subjective sense whereby, through our experience of nature's youthful spring and our own youthful love of another, all outside ourselves is briefly meaningful to us? [32] And, on the other hand, who created terror, madness, crime, remorse, lost hope, hate, self-contempt, pain, and the fear of hell? To the first two of these questions Demogorgon replies, "God: Almighty God" and "Merciful God." But unlike Anchises' replies to Aeneas, Demogorgon's is really no answer at all, and in place of the traditionally cryptic language of oracles he has substituted words that empty themselves of all meaning. For

[32]   Who made that sense which, when the winds of Spring
         In rarest visitation, or the voice
         Of one beloved heard in youth alone,
         Fills the faint eyes with falling tears . . .

         . . . .

         And leaves this peopled earth a solitude
         When it returns no more?   (II. iv. 12–18)

That this sense is the love whereby the self sympathizes and unites with the nonself to form the most vivid apprehension of "life" is further clarified by comparison with the essay *On Love:* "There is eloquence in the tongueless wind, and a melody in the flowing brooks and the rustling of the reeds beside them, which by their inconceivable relation to something within the soul, awaken the spirits to a dance of breathless rapture, and bring tears of mysterious tenderness to the eyes, like . . . the voice of one beloved singing to you alone. . . . So soon as this want or power is dead, man becomes a living sepulchre of himself, and what yet survives is the mere husk of what once he was."

when Asia then asks, "Whom calledst thou God?" he replies, "I spoke but as ye speak" (II. iv. 112). Shelley's
Demogorgon, who might have written the atheistic notes
to *Queen Mab*, has denied the validity of Asia's question.
Since there is no Creator, the only way to answer is to
use the language of those who think the question valid:
if you assume the world was created, then it was created
by its creator. Nor does Demogorgon really answer
Asia's third question, not because, like the first two, it
begs the question, but because the answer is inexpressible and incomprehensible by mind. All evil flows from
tyranny; and the answer to Asia's question is not necessarily "Jupiter," but "He reigns," since "To know nor
faith, nor love, nor law; to be / Omnipotent but friend-
less is to reign," as Asia herself explains (II. iv. 47–48).
"Omnipotent" is of course an ironic exaggeration, since
Jupiter is but a distorted and unreal projection of Prometheus, has no autonomous existence, and, although rain-
ing down evil, is himself the enslaved servant of evil.
The problem is the insoluble one of causation, for every
master of evil is slave to a master of evil, ad infinitum.
Jupiter is the "supreme of living things" (II. iv. 113)
only because at this moment he is master of the "world
of being," but his relation to the ultimate source of evil,
the final master who is not enslaved to yet a higher master, is that of the events of the living world to Demogorgon. Ultimate cause, the "deep truth" which would answer Asia's question, is "imageless" because Demogorgon
and his realm, being ontologically different from the "re-
volving world," are imageless, a formless darkness unavailable to the senses of the mind. Evil, then, is the
eternal potentiality of tyranny in the imageless Power
and can be released into actuality as a Jupiter by the
One Mind's yielding up its faculties and objectifying

them as an hypostatized institution; but it is released into actuality as an infinite chain of tyrannies, of which even the primaeval tyranny is an enslavement to evil, and behind that primaeval event the mind cannot see.

Like many of the other myths constitutively drawn into *Prometheus Unbound,* that of Virgil's sixth book has been remolded into what Shelley's imagination conceives to be the most nearly perfect shape of which it is capable, so that it may embody the truth that had eluded Virgil; and as a result Shelley's adaptation, although entirely independent of its source for its existence and meaning, ironically plays against it. Demogorgon has in no way supplied the theology that Anchises so freely expounded, for the idea of an oracular Anchises implies, in the context of the assumptions of Shelley's play, superstitious faith in an external source of supernatural revelation and makes possible institutional religions, built as they are on their claims to supernatural knowledge. Demogorgon's cave is "oracular" only in the sense that everything in actuality and time flows from the infinitely distant potentiality: what will happen in time is present in, although not occasioned by, the atemporal potentiality of time. But since mind cannot have experiential knowledge of that potentiality, it can only know that there are mysteries, not what they are. Mind, therefore, cannot gain knowledge from external institutions pretending to ultimate truths, but must derive its knowledge from itself, even though that self-examination reveals, skeptically, the mind's ignorance of what lies outside being. Lucretius, consistently scornful of oracles, had praised some philosophers because "in making many excellent and inspired discoveries [about physical nature] they have given responses as it were from the heart's adytum, with more sanctity and far more certainty than the Pythia who speaks forth from Apollo's tripod and laurels"; [33] and Asia adopts the words of this Epicurean poet in response to Demogorgon's failure to communicate oracular truths:

> So much I asked before, and my heart gave
> The response thou hast given; and of such truths
> Each to itself must be the oracle.[34]
>
> (II. iv. 121–23)

Nor indeed is Asia's final question answered in the terms in which she poses it. In the underworld Anchises has foreknowledge of the eventual return of the Golden Age under Augustus, not because there is any inevitability in the course of history nor because his foreknowledge affects that course, but simply because he has supernatural prescience of what has been arbitrarily decreed by Fate. But when Asia, knowing only that "Prometheus shall arise / Henceforth the sun of this rejoicing world," asks when that Golden Age will be, she is answered merely, "Behold!" (II. iv. 126–28). As infinite potentiality, Demogorgon is the infinity of that which enters actuality as time, and therefore all chronological time is present to him. The Hour who will bear Asia to Prometheus and restore the Golden Age "waits" for her in an ever-present now (II. iv. 141). In the rigorously causal world of Shelley's poem the answer to Asia's "When?" is "Behold!" because potentiality is ever wait-

---

[33] *De rerum natura* i. 736–39; see also Lucan *Pharsalia* ix. 564–65.
[34] This adaptation has been pointed out by Paul Turner, "Shelley and Lucretius," *RES*, n.s., X (1959), 275. What Lucretius meant to Shelley can be judged by his having adopted as the epigraph to *Queen Mab* the passage in which Lucretius announces that his poetic task is to set minds free from the knots of religious superstition. In the Preface to *The Revolt of Islam* he wrote that Lucretius' "doctrines are yet the basis of our metaphysical knowledge."

[139]

ing to be roused into act, and Love's quest for the Promethean Age makes that future event present.

IV

When Demogorgon then displays to Asia the future Hours, one of whom waits for her, she at first mistakenly believes hers is a "ghastly charioteer" in a "dark chariot." This, however, proves to be the Hour with whom Demogorgon, the "terrible shadow," will ascend to "wrap in lasting night heaven's kingless throne." Only after Demogorgon has risen in the dark chariot will Asia ascend in a brilliant one guided by an Hour with "the dove-like eyes of hope." This twofold pattern is recurrent throughout the play in many forms, and a collation of some instances will make evident its significance. It will be recalled that in Act I one of the Furies sang of the "disenchanted nation" that

> Springs like day from desolation;
> To truth its state is dedicate,
> And Freedom leads it forth, her mate;
> A legioned band of linked brothers
> Whom Love calls children—.

(I. 568–72)

Another Fury, knowing the cruelest pain it can inflict on Prometheus, breaks in to deny that these are the children of Love:

> 'Tis another's:
> See how kindred murder kin:
> 'Tis the vintage-time for death and sin:
> Blood, like new wine, bubbles within:
> 'Till Despair smothers
> The struggling world, which slaves and tyrants win.

(I. 572–77)

For Shelley means to drive home the truth that the revolutionary overthrow of tyranny does not of itself produce the Golden Age. By itself, it merely lays the ground for another political tyranny, just as the French Revolution had done: "Tyrants rushed in, and did divide the spoil" (I. 654). And, correspondingly, Christ's revolution, not being succeeded by a spirit of love, permitted the ecclesiastical tyranny that enslaved the freed. Asia's first bewildered belief that she is to rise in the chariot of Revolution is man's common mistake: the revolutionary withdrawal of evil is not the work of Love but is aroused by it and must be followed immediately by it.

This simple formulation—the retraction of evil by Demogorgon upon being awakened by Love, and the immediate release and guarantee of the "natural" order of events by Love—is the heart of Shelley's millennial vision. It obviously accounts for the large design of his narrative: Prometheus' revolutionary withdrawal of his curse in winter is directly followed by the journey of Love to Demogorgon's realm at the very moment of spring; and Demogorgon's revolutionary flight to withdraw Jupiter is immediately followed by Love's flight to reunion with Prometheus. The same pattern explains why, when men in their rebellious, enthusiastic youth drink the oracular vapors of Demogorgon's cave and "call" it truth, virtue, and love, their maddened, Maenad-like response is a "contagion to the world" (II. iii. 10). As Shelley wrote elsewhere, the revolutionary upsurge of the spirit of liberty is a "glorious madness" that pours abroad like a "wide contagion," [35] but a madness nevertheless, a mere chaotic wildness without love. The formula similarly explains why, when the primitive Gaia was priestess of the Delphic oracle, she inspired the "err-

[35] *Revolt of Islam*, IX, iv–v.

ing nations round to mutual war, / And faithless faith,"
while now that Asia is restored to the liberated Prometheus the Themis-like oracle inspires "calm and happy
thoughts." But the gospel that Shelley is intent on
preaching demands not only that Revolution be succeeded by Love but also that the succession be immediate. Hence in Act I the first of the consoling Spirits of the
Human Mind, representing Revolution and flying to Prometheus on "a battle-trumpet's blast," tells that when religious and political tyranny were overthrown and the
first exultant cry, "Freedom! Hope! Death! Victory!" had
faded,

> one sound, above, around,
> One sound beneath, around, above,
> Was moving; 'twas the soul of love.
>
> (I. 703–5)

Thus, despite Asia's impatience, the flight of the Hour
bearing her to Prometheus takes place with the utmost
speed (II. v. 6–7) because, unnatural evil having been
removed, the Hour of Love must succeed the Hour
of Revolution in the realm of mind with the same unrelenting haste that, as Panthea's and Asia's dreams of Necessity had revealed, takes place in the will-less physical
world. What Panthea and Asia had seen was that the almond tree and the new grass of spring hasten to burgeon
even before the old winter that would destroy them
has faded; and Asia impatiently follows Demogorgon into the realm of being as immediately as the symbolic morning of her flight succeeds the symbolic night
of his.

CHAPTER IV

❧ THE BREATHING EARTH ❧

IT WILL be useful at this point to summarize the structure of the play's metaphysics as it has emerged in these chapters. As the One Mind, Prometheus is identical with Being, or Life, and is limited to its scope and capabilities. Only in his possessing will can he be said to have power, and it is a power only to consent or refuse to yield control over that will to anything outside himself. He is free to resist the effort of tyranny to bend his will and free to relinquish his will to Necessity, but he has no causal power. Human minds are a mode of this absolute being, but since they are only portions of the One Mind and are subject to the illusions of time, space, and mutability, the imaged reality they constitute is only appearance, a deluding "veil which those who live call life." Jupiter also, we have noted, is but a function of Prometheus, a feigned distortion of the One Mind projected by it upon a feigned Heaven and, in turn, disfiguring the realm of being by its despotism. Even though Jupiter is eventually withdrawn from being to Demogorgon's realm, he is to remain there as a potential condition, not an independent reality. Prometheus, Jupiter, Asia, and the human mind represent only Being, its possible modes, and its possible factors; they can only affect events, not effect them. Within this realm of being, the principle governing the processes of events is Demogorgon's inviolable law of Necessity—quite independent of Prometheus' will—according to which what is called a cause must be followed by what is called a determined effect. However, these patterns of succession are the laws of the Power's manifestations within the realm of being, not the causative Power itself. Strictly speaking, then, there are only two self-sustaining factors in the drama: Prometheus, the One Mind, or Being, and Demogorgon, absolutely different from the One Mind and inaccessibly remote from it and yet the mysterious source of all the energy that appears in the domain of the One Mind as the sequences of events.

In *Mont Blanc* Shelley had placed this unknowable cause where it is traditionally conceived to be, transcendently above the world, and he had symbolized it as the perpetual falling of the gleaming snow on the mountain peak. The transcendent region of the Power is the qualityless and thus inexperienceable absolute of all those sensible qualities that it evolves into in the world of human experience; and the mutating form that flows from it—snow, glacier, and river—pursues its downward course through the sensible world according to the law of Necessity. In *Adonais,* where the subject is not being, as it is in *Prometheus Unbound,* but the meaning of death and the postmortal existence of the human soul, the perfect One, or the Truth-Beauty-Goodness from which the human soul derives and to which it returns, is also imaged transcendently as the heavenly sun and its attendant stars. Perfection is felt to be "above," as it is in the Christian cosmology; and the desired journey of the soul is an ascent, whereas the belief that death is a descent ("where all things wise and fair / Descend") is represented as arising from a mistaken theology or as true only of the material body ("Dust to the dust! but the pure spirit shall flow / Back to the burning fountain whence it came"). But in *Prometheus Unbound* the unitary perfection, Truth-Beauty-Goodness, although assumed in the philosophic content, is not an operative factor in the drama, which is acted out on other grounds and in other terms. Here not only does Shelley evade the question of death and the postmortal existence of the human soul, nudging it beyond the concerns of the play with only a hint of his speculations; [1] he also is occupied with overthrowing the assumptions of conventional theologies. Consequently, he inverts the usual theological values of "above" and "below," for if the transcendent God of the theologians is an anthropomorphic projection that tyrannizes over its fabricator, then superiority of place is symbolic of tyranny over the spatially inferior. The only occupants of Shelley's spatial Heaven are Jupiter and his co-operating gods because superiority is the spatial symbol of the suppressor. Ideally, Heaven should not be occupied at all; a republic is the equality of place —"Eldest of things, divine Equality!" [2] In fashioning his Jupiter Shelley has erased all distinction between the heavenly God of Christianity and the Satanic prince of the power of air who, in consequence of ruling "on high" (I. 281), can rain down plague and evil (I. 172, 266; II. iv. 100), send down his mischiefs from his "etherial tower" (I. 274–75), and cause confusion and all manners of pain to fall on man from heaven (I. 652; II. iv. 50–52). [3] Not simply because of Aeschylus' myth but

[1] E.g., III. iii. 108–12.　　[2] *Revolt of Islam,* V. song iii. 1.
[3] Compare Eph. 2:2.

also because of this symbolic significance of height, the punishment meted out to Prometheus is enchainment to a barren precipice in the Caucasus, where he longingly reminisces on the "o'ershadowing woods" of the ravine below, through which he had once wandered in union with Asia (I. 122). As Shelley formulates it, the history of Prometheus' restoration is his movement from bound exposure on the barren mountain height—"Black, wintry, dead, unmeasured; without herb, / Insect, or beast, or shape and sound of life"—to the freedom of the luxuriant, enclosing cave.

It is the characteristic of Shelley's imagination that he conceived of a great many of his poems in cosmic terms, postulating in them an entire universe, together with its spiritual physics. Indeed, the cosmic scope almost necessarily follows from his theory of the relation of mind to what we call the external universe. *The Sensitive Plant*, for example, supposes a total world consisting of a universal garden, the Lady who is the existing power of its existence, and man, the sensitive plant; and the poem reveals that ideally the world-garden is a mirror image of the eternal star-covered sky. *Mont Blanc*, which defines the universe in terms of the presence of images in the mind ("The everlasting universe of things / Flows through the mind"), fashions a total metaphysical world out of the mountain and its ravine, and develops into a symbolic physics the evolution of the glaciers and then the river from the snow on the mountain peak. In *Epipsychidion* the poet expressly defines himself as an earth controlled by the spiritual forces of a sun, a moon, and the Morning-Evening Star. And not only does much of the poetic activity of *Adonais* center in the elaborate symbolism of the world-enveloping atmosphere, but at one point the mourner is even directed to identify himself with the globe of the earth. These same cosmic dimensions are present in *Prometheus Unbound,* where, rejecting a world presided over from above as necessarily enslaved, Shelley has substituted a world, symbolic of the total realm of existence, whose actuating source is beneath, a world diffusing from its infinitely remote center. It is a world whose potentialities for perfection—and therefore its "divinity"—are within, not one in which all is imposed from without. For in denying a superior Creator and Governor, Shelley has really transferred the mysterious ultimate cause to the inaccessible and unknowable interior of the mind and of the universe that is by virtue of mind, just as in his *Defence of Poetry* he was to write of "the divinity in man" and to attribute the poet's momentary intuitions of perfect form not to any transcendent Idea (despite what the Platonizers of Shelley may claim), but to submission to a power seated upon the throne of the soul and arising, as he says, "from within."

II

Behind the world-structure and spatial organization that govern his drama lies Shelley's adaptation of the Renaissance conceptions of "meteorology," the science of "all natural processes that occur in the Region of Air: clouds, dew, winds, lightning, comets, rainbows, and associated weather processes." [4] All these diverse atmos-

[4] S. K. Heninger, *A Handbook of Renaissance Meteorology* (Durham, N.C., 1960), p. 4. Despite Shelley's obvious interest in science, it is quite mistaken, as a poem like *Adonais* testifies, to believe that it prevented him from exploiting all exploded scientific theories and fantasies for the purpose of poetic conception and expression, and thus to search only among the latest scientific findings of his day for the clues to his imagery.

pheric events are bound together by the doctrine, rooted in classical science and still governing much of the scientific vision and vocabulary of Shelley's day, that "meteors" are "exhalations," whether breathed out or drawn up from the surface and interior of the earth. The picture created by this science and adopted by Shelley in his drama is of a world repeatedly breathing out dew, vapor, mist, clouds, earthquakes, and volcanic eruptions. All fiery, glowing meteors are enkindled exhalations of the earth; plague is a noxious exhalation from the earth that spreads through the air by contagion; a flower's exhalation is its scent; even the vegetation that springs from the earth may be thought of in these terms, so that the buried corpse "Exhales itself in flowers of gentle breath." [5] More than metaphorically, the earth is, as Shelley records in *Prometheus Unbound*, "the breathing earth" (II. ii. 52), the ultimate source of its exhalations lying immeasurably and impenetrably deep within itself.

But although the poem rejects a supervisory God as necessarily evil, the world Shelley pictures as dynamically exhaling and diffusing from a Power at its unimaginable center is not necessarily, because of this fact, a good. The hypothesis only provides Shelley with a cosmic metaphor for the true relation of the Power to the realm of being and rejects the fictitious spatial relationships on which tyranny is founded; it is ethically neutral, merely describing the operations of the universe, not evaluating them. For the Power and its law of Necessity fulfill themselves indifferently, without regard to any teleology, so that in *Mont Blanc,* for example, it is merely in accordance with the neutral law of Necessity that the snow by which the Power manifests itself becomes the glaciers and they in turn become the river. That the gla-

[5] *Adonais,* 173.

ciers are murderous to man and the rivers life-giving is not the consequence of any intention of the Power, which is incapable of intent; it is an inescapable fact to which man must adapt himself. In this context good and bad are values relevant to mind alone and describe the ways in which it responds to the Power and its laws: "We are taught by the doctrine of Necessity that there is neither good nor evil in the universe, otherwise than as the events to which we apply these epithets have relation to our own peculiar mode of being." [6] We are expected to take Jupiter at his word when, overcome by Demogorgon and finding he can beg from this Power no mercy, pity, release, or respite, he contrasts him with Prometheus, who "would not doom me thus. / Gentle, and just, and dreadless, is he not / The monarch of the world?" (III. i. 67–69). Passion, virtue, and will are exclusively the attributes of mind, and by means of them it determines and rules over the world it constitutes. But of Demogorgon, Jupiter can only ask, "What then art thou?" (III. i. 69), since no mental terms are applicable to the mysterious Cause that acts according to fixed laws, without emotion, evaluation, purpose, or choice. What Shelley had written earlier of Necessity applies equally to the Power from which it derives:

> all that the wide world contains
> Are but thy passive instruments, and thou
> Regard'st them all with an impartial eye,
> Whose joy or pain thy nature cannot feel,
> Because thou hast not human sense,
> Because thou art not human mind.
>
> (*Queen Mab*, VI. 214–19)

At this stage of his thought Shelley can be considered a Manichaean only in a highly qualified sense. No longer

[6] Note to *Queen Mab* on "Necessity."

does he suggest, as he did in *The Revolt of Islam,* belief in a perpetual struggle between two independent forces, each of which conquers alternately. Rather, he now assumes that both good and evil are potentials, and that the potentiality of evil is suppressed and made inert, but not destroyed, by the natural and unobstructed functioning of the laws of the universe. This relation of nature to evil Shelley was to symbolize, somewhat inadequately, in *The Sensitive Plant,* by means of the Venus-like sustaining Spirit's care of the world-garden:

> And all killing insects and gnawing worms,
> And things of obscene and unlovely forms,
> She bore, in a basket of Indian woof,
> Into the rough woods far aloof,—
>
> In a basket, of grasses and wild-flowers full,
> The freshest her gentle hands could pull
> For the poor banished insects, whose intent,
> Although they did ill, was innocent.   (II. 41–48)

But, however much these lines may strive, by describing the insects' intent as "innocent," to assert that "there is neither good nor evil in the universe, otherwise than as the events to which we apply these epithets have relation to our own peculiar mode of being," they tend to imply that "evil" is an actuality that must be banished, rather than a potentiality that must be suppressed. Not only must mind adapt itself to the indifferent Necessity, but moral evil, Shelley assumes in *Prometheus Unbound,* is only the mental distortion or contamination of the operations of Necessity, and this will-created evil can be withdrawn by the willful submission of the mind to the free and natural functioning of Necessity. Yet if this proposition denies the independent actuality of moral evil, it implies no sentimental optimism; Shelley recognizes evil, in this negative sense, as a continuous and powerful possibility that must be reined in, not merely banished, as the Lady of *The Sensitive Plant* far too gently and compassionately banished evil from the garden. Jupiter, that distortion of the natural called "evil," can be removed from actuality only by being suppressed into the center of potentiality, whence he forever threatens to erupt again.

On the cosmic scale of *Prometheus Unbound* the ethics outlined here is embodied in the dominant symbol of the breathing earth. Since the ethics of Shelley's symbolism provides that the will must permit the "natural" to diffuse itself from the central Power and must create the condition that will contract the noxious into its sleeping potentiality, the action of the play begins, not with Prometheus' canceling or destroying the curse, but with the request that it be shaped into palpable thought by words so that he may "recall" it—not merely remember, but literally draw it back to himself.[7] In accordance with the symbol of meteorological exhalations, he had once "breathed" the vengeful curse on Jupiter (I. 59) and would now retract, withdraw, that exhalation to its center of origin, just as in *Mont Blanc* the Power and its laws manifest in the mountain can "repeal" (in its etymological sense) large codes of fraud and woe, or just as Shelley will later pray that "the pale name of PRIEST might shrink and dwindle / Into the hell from which it first was hurled."[8] For the curse Prometheus had "breathed" on Jupiter, like this volcanic hurling forth of the name of priest, is represented as a volcanic eruption

[7] For some dissenting interpretations of "recall" (I. 59), see London *TLS*, December 16, 1955, p. 761; January 6, 1956, p. 7; January 20, 1956, p. 37.
[8] *Ode to Liberty*, 229–30.

whose exhalation shook the mountains and seas, split the air, and darkened the sky with glowing volcanic ash and smoke, until "there stood / Darkness o'er the day like blood" (I. 101–2). Prometheus now wills that the evil exhaled into actuality be contracted into the innocuous, dormant potentiality from which it had erupted, even as Jupiter himself will, in consequence, be retracted from heaven into the infinite depths of Demogorgon's cave. For the ethical corollary of this cosmic symbolism is that the atmosphere enveloping the world is not imposed from without but is the breath exhaled from its core: there is no source of its circumambient condition but its own remote depth, and therefore the meteorology of exhalation perfectly symbolizes the self-defining moral climate, determined as it is, not by superimposed codes but by the manner in which the emanation of Power is received into the realm of being. The perfect model of this ethics is the world, exhaling, as was believed, its own atmosphere, the enclosing sphere of vapor, or "steam," that is responsible for the world's weather. Virtue is the free effluence that benignly contains and enfolds that from whose heart it has arisen; evil, or tyranny, is an emanation that, by being received unnaturally into being, divides itself from it and enslaves and distorts it from without. The autonomy of the symbolic sphere that both diffuses from its mysterious center and thus embraces itself is radical to all of Shelley's thought and to his rejection of all imposed codes: "Each [life, or being] is at once the centre and the circumference, the point to which all things are referred, and the line within which all things are contained." [9]

For example, as Shelley was to write in his *Ode to Liberty*, words, being an exhalation of the mind, may

[9] *On Life.*

> make the thoughts obscure
> From which they spring, as clouds of glimmering dew
> From a white lake blot Heaven's blue portraiture.
>
> (234–36)

Similarly, because of that distortion which is hate, Earth, in accordance with the meteorological symbol, breathes forth an atmospheric plague that, in turn, infects her because it envelops her (I. 177–79). On the other hand, the transfigurations of both Asia and Prometheus are self-envelopments in their own exhalations of light. From within Prometheus love "Steamed forth like vaporous fire" (II. i. 75), and he was

> arrayed
> In the soft light of his own smiles, which spread
> Like radiance from the cloud-surrounded moon.[10]
>
> (II. i. 120–22)

At Asia's birth, and again at her spiritual rebirth, love burst from her "like the atmosphere / Of the sun's fire" (II. v. 26–27); she is shrouded in her own "atmosphere" of radiance (II. v. 54–59), and her own voice "folds" her from sight (II. v. 61–63). So, too, in the rhapsodic celebration of Act IV, Earth's joy is a "vaporous exultation" that springs from within and, she says, "wraps me, like an atmosphere of light, / And bears me as a cloud is borne by its own wind" (IV. 323–24); and love, springing up "from its awful throne of patient power / In the wise heart, . . . folds over the world its healing wings" (IV. 557–61).

---

[10] Shelley frequently conceives of smiles and laughter as a source of light. Doubtless he was influenced by the Latin practice of using *ridere* to mean "shine." See, e.g., Lucretius iii. 22, iv. 1125; Horace *Carm.* iv. 11. 6.

III

According to this symbolic cosmology, then, the "deep" can exhale either evil or the force which removes evil; it can be either hell or the heart from which the Golden Age emanates. And hence the brilliant propriety of Shelley's electing Demogorgon as the mythic representative of what Mary Shelley called "the Primal Power of the world." In Boccaccio's *De genealogia deorum,* which directly or at second hand almost certainly must have been the main source of Shelley's information,[11] it is explained that the simple rustics once believed that the absolutely primal (*a nemine genitum*) and eternal father of all things must be concealed in the bowels of the earth because they observed that all vegetation springs out of the ground, volcanoes vomit flames, caverns breathe forth winds, the earth quakes and emits bellows, and from its bowels are poured the waters. For these reasons, Boccaccio continues, the rustics believed that from the core of the earth volcanic eruptions had spewed forth the air, the seas, and the fires that became the sun, moon, and stars. Imagining, therefore, that there must be some dark, divine intelligence in the bowels of the earth, they thought it to be Demogorgon. Subsequent mythographers, of course, recognized the likelihood that Demogorgon is to be understood as the Pla-

[11] Shelley demonstrably had more information about Boccaccio's Demogorgon than was available to him in Peacock's note to his *Rhododaphne,* usually considered the source of his knowledge. Certainly Boccaccio's treatise must have been as accessible to him as it was to Peacock, and he could have found much of Boccaccio's account of Demogorgon summarized in the notes to a number of editions of classical works, such as Lucan's *Pharsalia* and Statius' *Thebaid.* Coleridge, incidentally, knew the Italian version of the *De genealogia* and in 1803 copied into

tonic or Stoic Demiurge.[12] Shelley's representation of
Power as the deep chthonian source of exhalations already had a precedent in myth, and his adaptation of
Demogorgon therefore is in accord with the complex
mythopoeic syncretism of the play. Moreover, according
to Boccaccio, Demogorgon sent from the bowels of the
earth not only its surface but also the heavenly bodies
and the surrounding air and sky; and thus the given
myth exactly accommodates itself to Shelley's recurrent
symbol of a world whose defining environment arises
from its own mysterious depths, not by imposition from
above. Even Boccaccio's description of Demogorgon as
sluggish, sleepy, and surrounded by mists and fog
lends itself to Shelley's conception of the ultimate Power
as a dormant potentiality which, being inaccessible to
the senses, can be represented only as "a mighty
darkness . . . / Ungazed upon and shapeless," having
"neither limb, / Nor form, nor outline." But Boccaccio
tells that he was led to descend into Demogorgon's underworld by his search for the one true God, first cause
of all things, and the express purpose of his chapter on
Demogorgon, father and chief of all the gods of the
gentiles, was to ridicule this foolish pagan superstition
and to oppose to this false earth-deity the true God of

his notebook a sentence from the description of Demogorgon (*Notebooks*, ed. K. Coburn [New York, 1957], items 1649, 1653; see also
2512, 2737).

For Joseph Harpur's early nineteenth-century interpretation of Demogorgon as the "unknown and incomprehensible energies of nature,
all depending on the eternal and necessary relations and aptitudes of
things," see Albert J. Kuhn, "Shelley's Demogorgon and Eternal Necessity," *MLN*, LXXIV (1959), 596–99.

[12] E.g., Lucan, *Pharsalia*, ed. Franciscus Oudendorpius (Leyden, 1728),
I, 497n, where Boccaccio's account is summarized and annotated. See
also Abbé Banier, *The Mythology and Fables of the Ancients*, II, 549,
where Demogorgon's name is etymologized as meaning "Genius or
Intelligence of the Earth."

Christianity, "qui in caelis habitat." Shelley's adoption
of Demogorgon not only exchanges the traditional values
of height and depth, transcendence and containment, but
inverts Boccaccio's Christian thesis by accepting the
pagan god whose existence Boccaccio had attributed to
the absence of Christian revelation and to the barbaric
ignorance that deified natural forces.

Like Boccaccio's figure, Shelley's Demogorgon is represented as volcanic, a fitting image of the Primal Power:
at about the time Shelley was beginning Act II he visited
Vesuvius and reported it to be "after the glaciers the
most impressive expression of the energies of nature I
ever saw. It has not the immeasurable greatness[,] the
overpowering magnificence, nor above all the radiant
beauty of the glaciers, but it has all their character of
tremendous & irresistible strength." [13] Not only does
Demogorgon overcome Jupiter in the manner of a volcanic eruption, but, as G. M. Matthews has perceptively
demonstrated, the descent of Asia and Panthea to
Demogorgon's realm in Act II is a journey into the crater
of a volcano.[14] Looking down from a pinnacle of rock
among the mountains, Panthea and Asia see Demogorgon's cave as "Like a volcano's meteor-breathing chasm"
and note the "crimson foam" of the vapor rising from it
(II. iii. 3, 18, 44). It is this volcanic imagery that allows
Shelley to place Boccaccio's volcanic Demogorgon in the
underworld of Virgil's sixth book and to send Panthea
and Asia on a journey that is an ironic adaptation of
Aeneas' descent to Anchises. For not only does Aeneas,

---

[13] Letter to Peacock, [17 or 18] December 1818 (*Letters*, ed. Jones, II, 62).

[14] I am greatly indebted to Mr. Matthews' "A Volcano's Voice in Shelley" (*ELH*, XXIV [1957], 191–228) for directing my attention to the
prevalence of the volcanic imagery in the poem. His study is, so to
speak, ground-breaking, both because of its findings and, I believe,
because of its critical assumptions about Shelley's poetry.

like these Oceanids, pass through a dark wood, but Avernus, where the Sibyl leads Aeneas into the underworld, was notable for its sulphurous exhalations [15] and was associated with the surrounding volcanic region.[16] In addition, the fact that the Sibyl leads Aeneas from the prophetic cave, where she is inspired by the rising exhalations, to the underworld entrance at mephitic Avernus corresponds to Panthea's description of the vapors rising from Demogorgon's volcanic cave as "oracular" (II. ii. 4).

But the foundation on which Shelley built his volcanic symbolism is not limited to traditional meteorology, the inversion of the Christian cosmology, Boccaccio's volcanic Demogorgon, and Book vi of the *Aeneid;* the volcano had also been present in an important way in the myth of Aeschylus' *Prometheus Bound.* At the height of his agonized defiance of Jove, Aeschylus' Prometheus aligns himself sympathetically with Jove's other rebellious victims:

Pity moved me, too, at the sight of the earth-born dweller
of the Cilician caves curbed by violence, that destructive

[15] *Aeneid* vi. 240–41; Lucretius, vi. 747–48.
[16] The Delphin Virgil (Ruaeus), for example, commenting on Avernus (*Aeneid* vi. 237), notes that not only the region of Cumae but the entire coast of Campania, like much of Sicily, is everywhere hollow, as is evident from Charybdis and from Vesuvius and Aetna, the fire-breathing mountains (*montibus ignivomis*).
But Shelley's knowledge of this region was not merely literary. In the first half of December, 1818, after Act I of *Prometheus Unbound* was completed but apparently before Act II was begun, he toured "the Mare Morto & the Elysian fields, the spot on which Virgil places the scenery of the 6th Aeneid," entered a Sibyl's cave ("not Virgils Sybil") on the shore of Avernus, noted that nearby "a high hill called Monte Nuovo was thrown up by Volcanic fire," and visited nearby Vesuvius, whose volcanic activity he described elaborately and with awe in a letter to Peacock ([17 or 18] December 1818, and 23–24 January 1819). Not only did he have *Aeneid* vi in mind at about the time he was to begin Act II, but he was also vividly conscious of its volcanic setting.

monster of a hundred heads, impetuous Typhon. He withstood all the gods, hissing out terror with horrid jaws, while from his eyes lightened a hideous glare, as though he would storm amain the sovereignty of Zeus. But upon him came the unsleeping bolt of Zeus, the swooping levin brand with breath of flame, which smote him, frightened, from his high-worded vauntings; for, stricken to the very heart, he was burnt to ashes and his strength blasted from him by the lightning bolt. And now, a helpless and a sprawling bulk, he lies hard by the narrows of the sea, pressed down beneath the roots of Aetna; whilst on the topmost summit Hephaestus sits and hammers the molten ore. Thence there shall one day burst forth rivers of fire, with savage jaws devouring the level fields of Sicily, land of fair fruit—such boiling rage shall Typho, although charred by the blazing levin of Zeus, send spouting forth with hot jets of appalling, fire-breathing surge.[17]

By ironically inverting Aeschylus' play and its interpretation of Prometheus and Zeus, Shelley has in effect written a counter-sequel that, by recounting Demogorgon's eruptive removal of Jupiter, assumes the fulfillment of Prometheus' prophecy, which Aeschylus of course intended only as an expression of Prometheus' sinful pride and perverted theology.

Shelley is of Typhon's party, and inasmuch as he is reinterpreting the Prometheus myth as a corrective of Aeschylus, it is this allusion by Aeschylus to Typhon, whom almost every mythographer identified as the volcanic deity,[18] that syncretically collects to itself in

[17] 353ff.
[18] According to the scholiast on Pindar's first Pythian ode, every mountain notable for exhalations or eruptions contains Typhon. Sir William Drummond claimed that "The history of the rebellion and punishment of the Titans is nothing else than an allegorical account of volcanic eruptions" (*Herculanensia* [London, 1810], p. 47).

Shelley's play the network of cosmological and mythic materials embodying the image of the volcano. For Shelley has tacitly cast Demogorgon in the role of Typhon and the other volcanic giants or Titans who, like Prometheus, rebelled against Jove. In accordance with his consistent myth-making process, he has not fabricated a completely new myth dictated by the requirements of his theme but has fastened upon relationships already implicit among natural events and diverse myths in order to shape that myth which, in proportion as it approximates beautiful unity, embodies truth. For example, Asia's and Panthea's *descensus ad inferos* through a volcanic crater is not merely a restructuring of Aeneas' descent in a volcanic region into Hades, nor is it simply a conflation of this with the fact that Typhon lies beneath Aetna; it also, and at the same time, embodies Boccaccio's account of his own journey, in search of the first cause of things, to Demogorgon's realm in the entrails of the earth by passing through Taenarus, the entrance to Hades, or, Boccaccio adds, through volcanic Aetna.

The established myth tells that Typhon and his fellow giants, born of Earth and sprung from its lowest depths (*emissum ima de sede terrae*),[19] succeeded briefly in driving Jove down from heaven by casting up bolts of fire and huge rocks; and Apollodorus adds that Typhon succeeded in imprisoning Jove in the Corycian cave,[20] just as Shelley's Demogorgon will imprison Jupiter in his cave. Typhon, the myth continues, was then overcome by Jove and flung beneath Aetna, whence, struggling to rise again, he rebelliously continues to vomit flames and rocks into the heaven and cause the earth to quake,[21]

[19] Ovid *Metamorphoses* v. 321.   [20] *Bibliotheca* i. 6. 3.
[21] E.g., Pindar *Pythian* i; Ovid *Metamorphoses* v. 315ff. Silius Italicus, after describing the hot springs and sulphurous exhalations about the

even as Prometheus was chained for his revolt and persisted in his defiance. Indeed, not only did any volcanic eruption whatsoever come to suggest renewed revolt against Jupiter, but Typhon and the other volcanic Titans like Briareus, Aegeon, and Enceladus became allegorical personifications of rebellion against authority, especially that of God and monarch.[22] The volcanic giants, therefore, precisely suited Shelley's theme, and all that was needed to assimilate them to Demogorgon was to exchange the values traditionally assigned to rulers and rebellions. Bacon, for instance, coming close to Shelley's application of the myth, had read the story of Jupiter and Typhon (*sive Rebellis*) as meaning that when a king becomes tyrannical and assumes absolute and arbitrary power the injured state will rise in monstrous rebellion against the oppressor.[23]

Shelley has fully detailed the volcanic quality of

Campanian coast and connecting them with the underworld, attributes them to the panting breath of the buried Giants and adds that the Giant beneath volcanic Inarime, throwing up flames from his rebellious mouth (*rebelli ore*), seeks, if ever he is allowed to get free, to renew his war against Jupiter and the other gods. Whenever the volcanoes threaten to erupt, heaven grows pale (*Punica* xii. 113–51).

[22] E.g., Sandys's translation of Ovid (Oxford, 1632), pp. 190–91.

Dryden, *Astrea Redux,* 33–40:

> The Vulgar gull'd into Rebellion, arm'd,
> . . . .
> Thus when the bold *Typhoeus* scal'd the Sky,
> And forc'd great *Jove* from his own Heaven to fly,
> (What King, what Crown from Treasons reach is free,
> If *Jove* and *Heaven* can violated be?). . . .

Pope, *Dunciad,* IV. 63–67:

> But soon, ah soon Rebellion will commence,
> If Music meanly borrows aid from Sense:
> Strong in new Arms, lo! Giant Handel stands,
> Like bold Briareus, with a hundred hands;
> To stir, to rouze, to shake the Soul he comes.

[23] *De sapientia veterum.* See also Natalis Comes *Mythologiae* vi. 22.

Demogorgon's emergence to meet Jupiter in a Typhon-like combat. He is a darkly glowing cloud that

> floats
> Up from its throne, as may the lurid smoke
> Of earthquake-ruined cities o'er the sea.
> . . . .
> . . . watch its path among the stars
> Blackening the night!
>
> (II. iv. 150–55)

And in overwhelming Jupiter, Demogorgon hovers over him, again like a volcanic cloud, darkening his fall (III. i. 82–83). With this volcanic image in mind we can appreciate more fully the irony of Jupiter's anticipating an incarnation of his own offspring who will preserve his tyrannous reign and finding instead Demogorgon, who will remove him from his heavenly throne. We have already observed that, as a consequence of his perverted values, his exultant description of his union with Thetis is in fact an unintentionally hideous parody of the union of Prometheus and Asia, a description of destructive rape, not of fertile love—and that his faith that his off-spring can be eternally incarnate in Demogorgon's limbs betrays his evil ignorance of both his own nature and Demogorgon's. But in addition, just as he believes Demogorgon to be his own child, he mistakes the Hour's mythic chariot bringing volcanic Demogorgon for a chariot like his own, which, according to some versions of the Jupiter myth, was the cause of thunder and lightning. "Hear ye," he asks, "the thunder of the fiery wheels / Griding the winds?" (III. i. 47–48). There is indeed fire and thunderous sound, but it is the cleansing fire [24]

---

[24] Because fire was used for medical purification and because sulphur was customarily burned to fumigate the air, Shelley, it is evident, con-

and rumbling of earth's eruption from its core of Power, sent up to purge heaven, not the searing fire and thunder of punitive heaven (III. i. 66); [25] and Jupiter is right, in a sense that he does not recognize, when he asks,

> Feel'st thou not, O world,
> The earthquake of his chariot thundering up
> Olympus? (III. i. 49–51)

It is the crowning irony, therefore, that when he realizes that Demogorgon has triumphed over him Jupiter prays,

---

ceived of volcanic eruption and the vapors of the associated earthquake as capable of purifying and therefore as symbolic of the cleansing revolution. "I will arise," says Laon,

> and waken
> The multitude, and like a sulphurous hill,
> Which on a sudden from its snows has shaken
> The swoon of ages, it shall burst and fill
> The world with cleansing fire: it must, it will—
> It may not be restrained! . . .
> (*Revolt of Islam,* II. xiv. 1–6)

Later Cythna will promise:

> soon bright day will burst—even like a chasm
> Of fire, to burn the shrouds outworn and dead,
> Which wrap the world; a wide enthusiasm,
> To cleanse the fevered world as with an earthquake's spasm!
> (*Ibid.,* IX. v. 6–9)

This last passage combines the image of the cleansing volcano with a reference to the medical practice of burning the clothes of those dead of the plague. Compare also Earth's description of the restored world: "And long blue meteors cleansing the dull night" (III. iii. 117). For the practice of fumigating with sulphur as a ritual, see the end of *Odyssey* xxii; and for its use to dispel the plague, see Walter G. Bell, *The Great Plague in London in 1665* (London, 1951), and Charles F. Mullett, *The Bubonic Plague and England* (Lexington, Ky., 1956), which also reports that the infrequency of the plague in the region of Vesuvius had long been noted.

[25] Shelley would have found a symbolic battle between volcano and lightning in Aeschylus' *Seven against Thebes* (485ff.), where two heroes confront each other, the shield of one showing Typhon belching fire and smoke and that of the other, Zeus holding a bolt of lightning in his hand.

Let hell unlock
Its mounded oceans of tempestuous fire,
And whelm on them into the bottomless void
This desolated world, and thee, and me,
The conqueror and the conquered, and the wreck
Of that for which they combated.   (III. i. 74–79)

For a volcano has indeed erupted, though not from what
Jupiter, like the theologians, thinks of as the "hell" of
torments; it will withdraw the combatants into potentiality, not sink them into ruin; and the event will not destroy the wrecked world, but leave it free from the harm
of evil.

IV

That the single dominant image of the breathing
earth symbolizes such opposite values as the volcanic
disordering of the earth by Prometheus' curse and enchainment and also the revolutionary eruption that removes Jupiter is the heart of Shelley's management of
the image, for it allows the poem's symbolic cosmology
and its ethical hypothesis to coincide. Much of the theme
of the poem unfolds through exploitation of the various
modes of the single image of earthly exhalations:
volcanoes are catastrophic, but they also can stir the le-
thargic earth to action and to new forms; [26] volcanic ex-

---

[26] Compare *Revolt of Islam*, I. xxxviii. 7–9:

  when Hope's deep source in fullest flow
  Like earthquake did uplift the stagnant ocean
  Of human thoughts—mine shook beneath the wide emotion.

Incidentally, the word "emotion," modified as it is by the spatial word
"wide," effectively plays upon its etymological meaning. The relation
between volcanoes and earthquakes was, of course, thoroughly understood and generally assumed by Shelley. See also II. ii. 50–51 ("soft
emotion / Attracts, impels them"); and n. 48 below.

halations were traditionally thought to be a source of the plague, and yet their sulphurous fumes can also be conceived of as purifying, since sulphur was customarily burned to dispel the plague and since volcanic regions were thought to be free of the disease; and volcanic vapors can inspire mere frenzy or true prophecy, for the ancient prophetesses of the oracular caves uttered their prophecies in a state of madness. Violent volcanic eruption is the geological enactment of rebellion and revolution,[27] but it may overthrow evil or merely distort the earth and end the Golden Age of eternal spring. For all events of every sort in the realm of being are consequences of the exhalations of the remote and hidden Power. As Asia and Panthea are drawn, according to the laws of Necessity, to Demogorgon's volcano—the "fatal mountain" (II. ii. 62) because it contains *in posse* all the events that are to be—they pass through a vaporous volcanic region like the Phlegraean Fields around Avernus; and there the wings of the Oceanids are uplifted for flight, not by their own will, but by the steam exhaled from the "breathing earth"[28] (II. ii. 52) by the same volcanic Power to whose throne they are being drawn. In other words, although the manifestations of the cosmic Power have multiple forms, significances, and values, they are all various modes of the single act of chthonian exhalation; and therefore this relationship ex-

[27] "We are surrounded here in Pisa by revolutionary volcanoes, which as yet give more light than heat: the lava has not yet reached Tuscany" (Shelley to Peacock, 21 March 1821). Compare also *Mask of Anarchy*, stanza 89:

> And that slaughter to the Nation
> Shall steam up like inspiration,
> Eloquent, oracular;
> A volcano heard afar.

[28] Shelley first wrote, "steaming earth." He may well have owed the term "breathing earth" to Silius Italicus' "tellus suspirans," which describes the volcanic fields of the Campanian coast and their vaporous exhalations (*Punica* xii. 135–36).

actly corresponds to the relation Shelley understood between Power and the events it effects in the realm of being. Like the breathing earth, Power fulfills itself in a single fixed sequence through the realm of mind; but whether the series of events it projects into being act as cataclysms or purifications depends upon the way in which mind, together with its faculty of will, receives them into its domain. The dynamics of the poem's world is the precise symbol of the ethical drama; and if we add that the universe is to be defined as the mass of knowledge, no essential distinction can really be made between world and mind, science and ethics.

The opportunity to exploit the image of exhalation in different forms and contexts therefore provides Shelley with a means of elaborating the dialectic of his theme and of weaving a texture of ironies—a dialectic and an ironic texture that cut across the unilinear dramatic progress by causing sectors of the play to interact at the level of imagery. For example, the assignment of approximately the same volcanic image to different actors in the play sustains the fact that they are all modes of the One Mind. Prometheus breathed forth his curse on Jupiter in a volcanic and seismic cataclysm that thundered, rocked the world, and covered the day with darkness; and, in what appears to be retaliation, his enchainment by Jupiter also produced a vast volcanic exhalation with the same consequences:

> the sea
> Was lifted by strange tempest, and new fire
> From earthquake-rifted mountains of bright snow
> Shook its portentous hair [29] beneath Heaven's frown.
> (I. 165–68)

[29] The image of course derives from the etymology of "comet," the fiery meteor that was the traditional portent of disaster.

For if it is correct to understand Jupiter as but a distorted reflection of Prometheus, Prometheus is really self-tormented, and his volcanic curse against Jupiter is, in fact, the same as the volcanic disorder with which Jupiter tortures the shackled Titan. For the same reason, when Jupiter's Phantasm is called up from the depths "underneath the grave" (I. 197), it also erupts volcanically: as it appears, driven up on "direst storms" (I. 242), its sound "is of whirlwind underground, / Earthquake, and fire, and mountains cloven" (I. 231–32), and when it repeats Prometheus' curse, "the Heaven / Darkens above" (I. 256–57), as it had when Prometheus originally gave volcanic utterance to the curse (I. 102). Moreover, since Prometheus represents the totality of being, it is proper that his various modes make similar volcanic and seismic defiances of Jupiter. Hence at the human level the analogue of Prometheus' volcanic curse is the distinctly Typhon-like rebellion against Jupiter's tyranny by the soul of man, which, "like unextinguished fire, / Yet burns towards heaven with fierce reproach . . . / Hurling up insurrection" (III. i. 5–8), even as the analogue in the man-made world to the noxious volcanic cataclysm is the religion-inflamed city that "Vomits smoke in the bright air" (I. 552). Like Prometheus, the Earth, since she exists in consequence of being perceived by Prometheus, also breathed a curse on Jupiter, and, she explains, "the thin air, my breath, was stained / With the contagion of a mother's hate / Breathed on her child's destroyer" (I. 177–79). For the speech-breath of hate is analogous not only to the exhalation of Prometheus' curse but also to the earth's polluted, miasmal exhalations released by earthquake and spread through the air as contagious mists.[30] And just as Prometheus' curse

[30] The article on "plague" in Ephraim Chambers' *Cyclopaedia* may be

of hate only perpetuated his imprisonment by the tyrant he cursed, so Earth's curse of hate merely infected her own enveloping atmospheric breath.

On the other hand, since the poem's spatial metaphor provides for one central Power from which everything radiates out into actuality, it is the innocent and mild forms of exhalation that tend to symbolize the natural and beneficial. The Hours, for example, originate in Demogorgon's cave "below the deep" (II. iv. 140; IV. 60) and thus in the Eternity with which Demogorgon identifies himself (III. i. 52); and, like the Echoes shrinking back into their native caves, they return to subterranean Eternity when their "time" has passed (IV. 14). For Eternity is to sequential time as the Power is to all sequences in the realm of being; and thus the Hours describe their own rising from potentiality into actuality as the removal of the "figured curtain of sleep / Which covered our being and darkened our birth . . . below the deep" (IV. 58–60). By assigning to Asia the characteristics of Aphrodite Anadyomene, Shelley can also picture her birth as an "uprise" from the cloven sea (II. v. 22); and Prometheus' birth from Earth's bosom is likened to her exhalation of a divine nimbus, "a cloud / Of glory" (I. 157–58). In view of these beneficent forms

taken as typical of the entire tradition that attributes the plague to subterranean exhalations and associates it with earthquake: "The disorder is generally supposed to be communicated by the air. . . . Mr. [Robert] Boyle attributes plague principally to the effluvia or exhalations breathed into the atmosphere, from noxious minerals. . . . The air . . . is depraved in far more places than improved, by being impregnated with subterraneous expirations . . . since morbific causes operate more effectually than curative ones, it seems more than probable, that exhalations ascending from under ground, may produce pestilential fevers, and the plague itself. . . . It is probable, peculiar kinds of venomous exhalations may sometimes be emitted, especially after earthquakes. . . ."

Lucan (vi. 90–92) attributes to the exhalations of volcanic Typhon both plague and raging madness.

[167]

of exhalation in the drama, and especially in view of the curative cosmic effect of Demogorgon's volcanic eruption, we can better appreciate the reason why, at the end of the play, Earth tacitly abstracts from the legend of King Bladud and the healing springs of Bath to pattern an account of man's moral purification: evil will

> Leave Man, even as a leprous child is left,
> Who follows a sick beast to some warm cleft
> Of rocks, through which the might of healing springs is
> poured.
>
> (IV. 388–90)

Like the volcanic clouds of sulphur and the curative sulphur fumes used to purge the air, the thermal springs, geologically related to volcanoes, are exhalations that "owe their origin partly to the admixture of sulphurous particles, while the water . . . creeps through beds and mines of sulphur, &c. and partly to the fumes and vapours exhaling through the pores of the earth where sulphur is. . . ."[31]

Given, then, a cosmic center of potentiality which diffuses into actuality and retracts from it, and given the premise that these exhalations are violent or gentle, beneficent or disruptive, and disruptive of good or evil, depending entirely upon the manner in which actuality receives them, an ironic interplay can be set in motion among the occurrences of this spatial image. For example, at the very beginning of the drama Prometheus is tortured by the Jupiter-sent earthquake that wrenches the rivets in his wounds (I. 38–40); at the conclusion of the drama love awakens the dead to "breathe a spirit up from their obscurest bowers" and, like "a storm bursting its cloudy prison," erupts from the "lampless caves" of

[31] Chambers' *Cyclopaedia*, art. "Bath."

Demogorgon's " unimagined being" to produce an earthquake that shocks thought's chaos out of its stagnation
(IV. 375–80). Similarly, Prometheus' volcanic curse on
Jupiter, like the Earth's, stands in ironic juxtaposition to
Demogorgon's volcanic flight to Jupiter: uttered in hate,
the curse was an eruption that merely perpetuated Jupiter's reign and distorted its speaker and his Earth; the
flight, aroused by Love, burst forth to recall Jupiter from
actuality. And whereas the Earth's curse of hate was a
self-infecting plague, upon the restoration of Prometheus
Earth can prophesy that instead of the nightly miasma
that is unwholesome to man and blights the flowers with
mildew, the exhalations of

> The dew-mists of my sunless sleep shall float
> Under the stars like balm: night-folded flowers
> Shall suck unwithering hues in their repose.
>
> (III. iii. 100–2)

Because the image of exhalation and the spatial pattern it implies are radical to the cosmos assumed by the
play, even the larger units of the action assume similar
designs so as to evaluate and comment on each other.
Thus Asia's descent into the realm of Power and her
arousing of Demogorgon to an eruptive violence that
topples Jupiter is the heroic version of the earlier deeds
of Mercury and the Furies in Act I; for the movements of
Mercury and the Furies describe the same spatial pattern as those of Asia and Demogorgon and seem a gruesome anticipatory travesty of them, in the same manner
that the union of Jupiter and Thetis horribly travesties
that of Prometheus and Asia. Not drawn down by the
natural processes of Necessity, as Asia is, but "driven
down" from Heaven by the tyrannical will of Jupiter, the
messenger of the gods calls up the monsters from "the

deep" (I. 462) to torture and subdue Prometheus—an anticipation of the time when Asia, Prometheus' messenger, will descend to rouse Demogorgon from the deep to rid Heaven of Jupiter. The "monster-teeming Hell" from which the Furies rise is "the all-miscreative brain of Jove" (I. 447–48), for they are fictitious distortions formed by the fictitious supreme tyrant and allowed by the One Mind to act as tormenting psychological realities. Inasmuch as organized religion and political despotism are a distortion of truth, this cosmic structure of a Hell from which the Furies emerge is an ugly parody of the true and natural cosmos and its workings; and consequently the Furies, like Demogorgon, are represented as volcanic and seismic "powers" (I. 367). Ascending from the "abyss" (I. 370) like exhalations—"Like vapours steaming up behind" (I. 329)—they "climb the wind" (I. 327). Jupiter's descent to reward them with human groans and blood when, charioted on a "sulphurous cloud," he "bursts Heaven's bounds" (I. 333–34) ironically anticipates the descent on which volcanic Demogorgon will drag him. In the manner of volcanic clouds, the Furies blacken the dawn (I. 441) as they gather "in legions from the deep" (I. 462); "steaming up from Hell's wide gate," they "burthen the blasts of the atmosphere" (I. 518–19), just as the curse of hate breathed by Earth had infected her atmosphere; they "trample the sea" and "shake hills" with their screams of mirth when "cities sink howling in ruin" (I. 498–500); and Panthea complains of the volcanic thunder of their rising:

> These solid mountains quiver with the sound
> Even as the tremulous air; their shadows make
> The space within my plumes more black than night.
>
> (I. 522–24)

Further, whereas the disfiguring eruption of the Furies anticipates the cleansing eruption of Demogorgon, the corrective counterpart (short of Love) to the Furies, whom Jupiter summons to torment Prometheus, is the Spirits of the Human Mind, whom Earth summons as consoling angels to this tortured Christ. The Furies erupt from the hellish abyss of Jupiter's misshaping brain, climb with clanging wings like steaming vapors, and call for aid from their fellows who reside in the human mind in the form of hatred and self-contempt and whose uprising makes "solid mountains quiver" (I. 522). The consolatory Spirits, by contrast, ascend gently from their "homes . . . the dim caves of human thought," rising "Like fountain-vapours when the winds are dumb" and "Thronging in the blue air" "Like flocks of clouds in spring's delightful weather" (I. 659–67). In accordance with Shelley's definition of the "universe," the metaphor identifies the human mind as a world that exhales these beneficent Spirits from its obscure inmost center. Hence Earth's statement that the "homes" of these Spirits are "the dim caves of human thought" and yet that they "inhabit, as birds wing the wind," thought's "world-surrounding ether" (I. 659–61), however inconsistent it has appeared to some critics, is wholly coherent if we recognize that these Spirits are imaged as vaporous exhalations and if we assimilate the image to the poem's consistent cosmological symbolism. The caves, like Demogorgon's cave or like that of the Echoes, are the "homes" of human thought in the sense of source, or place of origin; but once diffused, the Spirits inhabit the surrounding and defining atmosphere of the mind-world, just as birds on leaving their nests inhabit the air, or as earth's exhalations inhabit "cloudlike" the embracing atmosphere (I. 688). The mind, according to the recur-

rent symbol of the self-conditioning sphere, contains a
center that radiates to form the mind's own guarding and
consolatory ambience. Opposed to the volcanic Furies,
who, "steaming up from Hell's wide gate, . . . burthen
the blasts of the atmosphere," the mind's consoling Spirits
wing the surrounding atmosphere not only when it is
clear but even when it is laden with the mind's dark and
pestilential exhalations of evil:

> And we breathe, and sicken not,
> The atmosphere of human thought:
> Be it dim, and dank, and grey,
> Like a storm-extinguished day,
> Travelled o'er by dying gleams;
>   Be it bright as all between
> Cloudless skies and windless streams.
>
> (I. 675–81)

Moreover, this metaphor continues, by inhabiting
thought's encircling atmosphere, the Spirits of the Human Mind can "behold / Beyond that twilight realm, as
in a glass, / The future" (I. 661–63). Rejecting the concept of prophecy as supernatural revelation, Shelley defined it as foresight of the rigorously determined consequences inherent in any present event, according to the
doctrine of Necessity. The poet, for example, is prophet
only in that he "beholds the future in the present," [32] for
the present must evolve into the future by way of a fixed
pattern of succession. Since twilight is actually the atmospheric refraction of the light of the unseen sun
below the horizon, the Spirits, having emanated from the
center of the mind-world, can perceive in its immediate
and self-formed ambience, as in a mirror, the reflection
of the light that must necessarily be rising.

[32] *Defence of Poetry.*

The prophetic cave is an obvious adjunct of the volcanic metaphor, since the oracular priestess was inspired by the vapors rising from the volcanic crevices; [33] and Shelley employs these related geological symbols in related ways. Even apart from the geological connection between volcanoes and the *fatidici specus*, there is a logical relation between the two in Shelley's symbolic system, for if volcanic Demogorgon is the primal cause that manifests itself in actuality according to the laws of Necessity, and if all of the future is therefore inherent in Demogorgon's realm of absolute potentiality, then the vaporous chthonian exhalations are prophetic. Moreover, Lucan, who is one of the sources for Demogorgon, also accepted the Stoic belief that a great part of total divinity (*totius Jovis*) rules the world from within it and identified this Typhon- and Demogorgon-like divinity with the omniscient source of the vapors breathed forth in the oracular caves.[34] Hence it is consistent with the world structure framed by Shelley that Demogorgon be the source of both volcanic eruptions and oracular vapors. When, for example, Asia consults Demogorgon as an oracle and asks for those ultimate truths that reside

[33] Lucan, for example, describes the Delphic oracle as a huge chasm that breathes out divine truth and exhales speaking winds (*ventos loquaces*); and he compares the inspired priestess' utterance to the eruption of Aetna and to the howling of Typhon beneath his volcano (*Pharsalia* v. 82–101).

[34] *Pharsalia* v. 86–96. The commentators took it that Lucan was referring specifically to Demogorgon. Not unexpectedly, this doctrine of Lucan's was associated by the commentators (e.g., Cornelius Schrevelius in his edition of *De bello civili* [Amsterdam, 1658], p. 211n) with those lines in *Aeneid* vi which account for the Platonic or Stoic *anima mundi* and which had considerable formative influence on Shelley's presentation of Demogorgon in his Virgilian Act II (*Spiritus intus alit, totamque infusa per artus / mens agitat molem*). Banier, arguing that Demogorgon represents the earth's vegetative principle, also associates him with these lines by Virgil (*The Mythology and Fables of the Ancients* [London, 1740], II, 551).

exclusively, like Demogorgon himself, in the "unimagined" realm outside perceptible being, he replies not only in the cryptic manner characteristic of oracles, but also in a volcanic metaphor:

> If the abysm
> Could vomit forth [35] its secrets. But a voice
> Is wanting, the deep truth is imageless.
>
> (II. iv. 114–16)

Consequently, Shelley is careful to identify the volcanic with the oracular nature of Demogorgon's cave. Its mighty portal, Panthea says, is

> Like a volcano's meteor-breathing chasm,
> Whence the oracular vapour is hurled up [36]
> Which lonely men drink wandering in their youth,
> And call truth, virtue, love, genius, or joy,
> The maddening wine of life, whose dregs they drain
> To deep intoxication; and uplift,
> Like Maenads who cry loud, Evoe! Evoe!
> The voice which is contagion to the world.
>
> (II. iii. 3–10)

This elaborate metaphor of exhalations is carefully ambivalent, since the metaphor of a universe diffusing from a center is designed to imply in itself neither good nor evil and applies equally to the Furies and the Spirits of the Human Mind. The breath exhaled into the atmosphere because of the inspiring oracular vapors is potentially a pestilential contagion to the world like the plague breathed up by Earth in her hate; or, depending

---

[35] *Vomere* and *evomere* were the terms most frequently used by the Latin authors to describe volcanic action.

[36] Bodleian MS Shelley e.2, fol. 36ᵛ, reads, "breathed up," which better suits the idea of vapors. But the substitution of "hurled up" effectively fuses the image of the volcano with that of the oracular cave.

on the manner in which it is received, it may be a spreading, sanguine call for the overthrow of evil. The frenzied, Maenad-like state of youth's oracular intoxication [37] may produce drunken savagery like the French Revolution or, if it is immediately succeeded by mature Love, may revoke all that is not truth, virtue, love, genius, joy. The moral determinant is not the indifferent exhalations of Power, but the intemperate circumstance of reception implied by "youth." And, in accordance with this pattern, Earth's volcanic cave first "panted forth" her "spirit" as oracular vapors that merely maddened and lured to blind civil war while Jupiter determined the condition of being; but, with the liberation of the One Mind in the next age, its exhalation inspires "calm and happy thoughts" and feeds with its rich volcanic ash the lush vegetation of nature (III. iii. 135–46).

V

Because actuality is symbolized by "meteorological" diffusions from an inaccessible, cavernous world-center, and potentiality by containment in a cave, the course of the Promethean drama is developed as a series of symbolic ascents and descents, diffusions and retractions. Prometheus' "recall" of the curse he had volcanically breathed on Jupiter is succeeded in the next act by the withdrawal of Asia and Panthea into the volcanic center, where all potentiality resides. By virtue of Prometheus' retraction of the exhaled curse, the Oceanids are drawn by Necessity to trace sequentiality back to its origin in Demogorgon's cave, and therefore they are led by the

[37] Compare "Youth's smooth ocean, smiling to betray" (II. v. 100) and "the self-contempt implanted / In young spirits, sense-enchanted" (I. 510–11).

Echoes, not as they radiate out from their resonant center as sound, but as they recede into the cave, their traditional home, where they remain as silent, or sleeping, potentials of sound. Correspondingly, Demogorgon in his containing cave is the dormant volcanic potentiality whose "rest" Asia alone can break and awaken into active cause (II. i. 193). For in a significant sense Asia, as generative Love, is not only the companion of Being but also the earthly representative of the Power, since this "life of life" whose "footsteps pave the world / With loveliness" (II. i. 68–69) and whose "transforming presence" causes the flowers and grass to spring up (I. 827–33) is also causative, or at least is an agent of Cause. The love which is the generative spirit of "life" in the realm of being and which, like Demogorgon, is eternal and unaffected by "Fate, Time, Occasion, Chance, and Change" (II. iv. 119–20) obviously has affiliations, beyond the realm of being, with the primal Power of all such exhalations. It is for this reason that only Love, as messenger for Prometheus, can rouse the volcano from sleeping potentiality into the eruptive actuality which revokes the evil order and makes possible the release of the new. In logical sequence and in accord with the symbol of diffusion and retraction, Prometheus' recall of his volcanic curse is succeeded by Asia's withdrawal from actuality into Demogorgon's cave in order to rouse this sleeping Power behind all events to a volcanic eruption that, in subsiding, shrinks the transcendent Jupiter from actuality into the dormant center of potentiality, where he must dwell with Demogorgon "Henceforth in darkness" (III. i. 55–56). So also, Prometheus' total history, cast into these patterns of ascent and descent, is a spatial movement from the exposed height of a precipice in the Caucasus to Earth's oracular cave, like Demogor-

gon's, where he and Asia will be "unchanged" (III. iii.
24) and where the infinite Power will inspire these representations of perfect and absolute being with those
happy thoughts that are their "unexhausted spirits" (III.
iii. 36).

The withdrawal of Prometheus and Asia to their cave,
like the descent of Asia in Act II and the revocation of
Jupiter to Demogorgon's cave, is, then, a withdrawal
from the mutable actuality of space and time into the
containment of potentiality, which is the way in which
the play defines eternity, as Demogorgon's identification
of himself as Eternity makes clear. Recognition of the
temporal symbolism of this pattern of retreat will put
into meaningful focus Asia's otherwise curious song of
her withdrawal with Prometheus from human time after
their transfigurations:

> We have passed Age's icy caves,
> And Manhood's dark and tossing waves,
> And Youth's smooth ocean, smiling to betray:
> Beyond the glassy gulfs we flee
> Of shadow-peopled Infancy,
> Through Death and Birth, to a diviner day;
> A paradise of vaulted bowers,
> Lit by downward-gazing flowers.
>
> (II. v. 98–105)

Obviously Shelley has conceived of earthly life not as a
linear movement into birth and through death but as a
kind of cul-de-sac whose entrance, called "Death and
Birth," is also its exit.[38] The contradictory nature of the
imagery in these lines is designed to convey this fact; for
temporal life is represented as a passage inward, against

---

[38] Compare *Epipsychidion*, 379–80: "the star of Death / And Birth."
If Shelley is referring to Venus, as seems likely, the point is that the
Morning Star and the Evening Star are the same.

the flow of the water and through ever-narrowing and more forbidding waters to Age's icy caves, and death is a retreat along the flow of the water and from the cul-de-sac to eternity, like the retreat of Prometheus and Asia to their cave, of the Echoes to theirs, and of Asia and Panthea to Demogorgon's. Paradoxically, although the temporal movement of life, from youth to age, is imaged as passage from ocean to tempestuous river and then to icy cave, the metaphor in fact compels in the opposite direction, that is, from the cavernous source of the waters to the ocean into which they flow; and although the chronology of life leads to the icy caves of age, the retreat from time through constantly widening expanses of water ends, like Prometheus' retreat, not in infinite space but in the enclosing "paradise of vaulted bowers, / Lit by downward-gazing flowers" (II. v. 103–4) that symbolizes the eternity of contained potentiality.[39]

This controlling pattern of a cavernous container symbolizing potentiality and of diffusions from it symbolizing actuality defines the function of Proteus' shell, with which the Hour announces and disseminates the new age throughout the world after the reunion of Prometheus and Asia. For if the culmination of the drama is the retreat of the One Mind into the immutable eternity of the cave, it is also, inversely, the diffusion of perfection throughout the human, temporal world from the potentiality in which it has been contained. Shelley's choice of Proteus' "curved shell" as an analogue of the other caves of potentiality is one of his happiest mythopoeic findings and transformations. As a sea-god, Proteus can readily be drawn into the network of myths that includes the sea-born Venus-Asia, daughter of Ocean. And the traditional

[39] Compare the similar imagery in the description of Prometheus' cave (III. iii. 10–17).

interpretation of Proteus as the shapeless and ever-changing primal matter to whom primal nature had revealed all its secrets, including knowledge of past, present, and future, obviously entitles him to serve as a kind of surrogate in the realm of imaged being for Demogorgon, the shapeless, impalpable Cause in "unimagined" being.[40] Like Demogorgon, whose cave exhales oracular vapors, Proteus, having knowledge of all times, is notably the prophet; and like Demogorgon, the "Primal Power," Proteus was addressed in Thomas Taylor's translation of the Orphic hymn as "First-born," to whom "all things Nature first . . . consign'd." [41] Consequently, Proteus' shell is analogous at the human level to Demogorgon's cave at the level of the One Mind: each is the potentiality from which perfection is breathed out into actuality.[42] Apparently, it was Bacon's interpretation that most helped shape Shelley's conception of Proteus; [43] for Bacon also rejected the idea of supernatural prophecy, and the myth according to which Proteus divulges the future to anyone who can hold him fast he took to represent the necessary causal sequence in nature:

[40] For the traditional interpretations of Proteus, see A. B. Chambers, "Milton's Proteus and Satan's Visit to the Sun," *JEGP*, LXII (1963), 280–87.

[41] *The Hymns of Orpheus* (London, 1792), p. 149. In his edition of Milton's *Paradise Lost* ([London, 1750], I, 239n) Thomas Newton interpreted Proteus as "the first principle of things."

[42] For Shelley's interpretation of Proteus as the activating spirit of the world inhabited by man, see his *Essay on Christianity:* "[The God described by Christ] is neither the Proteus [n]or the Pan of the material world."

[43] *Triumph of Life*, 269–73:

> If Bacon's eagle spirit had not lept
> Like lightning out of darkness—he compelled
> The Proteus shape of Nature, as it slept
> To wake, and lead him to the caves that held
> The treasure of the secrets of its reign.

And whereas it is added in the fable that Proteus was a prophet and knew the three times; this agrees well with the nature of matter: for if a man knew the conditions, affections, and processes of matter, he would certainly comprehend the sum and general issue (for I do not say that his knowledge would extend to the parts and singularities) [44] of all things past, present, and to come.[45]

Most excellently therefore did the ancients represent Proteus, him of the many shapes, to be likewise a prophet triply great; as knowing the future, the past, and the secrets of the present. For he who knows the universal passions of matter and thereby knows what is possible to be, cannot help knowing likewise what has been, what is, and what will be, according to the sums of things.[46]

It is highly appropriate, therefore, that this primal spirit of nature should have given Asia the sea shell, Venus' traditional emblem, as a nuptial gift and should have breathed into it a "voice to be accomplished" (III. iii. 67), since the union of the One Mind and generative Love created a condition fraught with future consequences that must, "according to the sums of things," be fulfilled in the manner of prophecy, now that Asia and Prometheus are reunited. The shell into which Proteus breathed his prophecy so that it contained the sounds of the sea functions like Earth's oracular cave of Power, which, upon the return of Asia to Prometheus, exhales calm perfection; and just as Demogorgon in his cave is a sleeping voice "unspoken" until roused by Asia (II. i. 191), or as the "spell" treasured for Asia in that "remotest" cave is "Like veiled lightning asleep" (II. iii.

---

[44] Compare *Defence of Poetry:* "Not that I assert poets to be prophets in the gross sense of the word, or that they can foretell the form as surely as they foreknow the spirit of events. . . ."
[45] *De sapientia veterum,* xiii. [46] *Descriptio globi intellectualis,* v.

83), so the music confined in the shell is, as latent potentiality, "like lulled music sleeping" (III. iii. 73). Like
Asia when she stirred the sleeping, confined primal
Power into volcanic exhalation, the vernal Hour who
bore Asia from Demogorgon's cave and who symbolizes
the new order of time is to "breathe into the many-folded
shell, / Loosening its mighty music" [47] (III. iii. 80–81)
so that the cavernlike shell may exhale into human actuality the prophecy it contains. The imprisoned "voice to
be accomplished" is to be released by the Hour about
the earth like a revolutionary atmospheric disturbance
that it might reverberate like thunder (III. iii. 82; III.
iv. 98) and shake the startled world (III. iv. 54–55), and
thus correspond at the human level to the first event
bringing about the new Promethean age, Demogorgon's
revolutionary eruption. The revolutionary storm of the
shell's music clears the earth's atmosphere, just as Demogorgon's revocation of Jupiter had purged Heaven; and
the immediate succession of Demogorgon's chariot by
that of Asia, or Love, is repeated in the human domain,
for at once

> the impalpable thin air
> And the all-circling sunlight were transformed,
> As if the sense of love dissolved in them
> Had folded itself round the sphered world.
>
> (III. iv. 100–4)

The gift of potentiality honoring the union of the One
Mind and Love has been exhaled into the actuality of
human time as an embracing and world-determining atmosphere of love, corresponding to all the many other
symbolic sphere-enclosing atmospheres of the poem. The
corollary of the withdrawal of the One Mind with Love

---

[47] Compare the similar "many-folded mountains" (II. i. 201) within
which is the entrance to Demogorgon's cave.

into the cave of eternal and immutable perfection is the effusion of the "natural" perfection from its shell-cave throughout the world of human minds.

But although Shelley has so subtly and elaborately drawn on the myths of Venus, the Hora, and Proteus to fashion the symbolism of the prophetic shell from which the earthly millennium will flow, it is clear that he has done so in order to adapt it to his drama as a continuous reinterpretation of Scripture. For in assigning the shell to the Hour that she may breathe into it and loosen its "mighty music," Shelley has substituted the musical shell for the last trumpet, which will summon the dead to the Last Judgment so that the corruptible will put on incorruption and the mortal will put on immortality (I Thess. 4:16; I Cor. 15:52; Rev. 8:2 ff.). No New Jerusalem has supernaturally come down to earth "from God out of heaven," nor has immortality been divinely superadded to man; the perfection casually inherent in the union of Mind and Love has come to its necessary fruition, and man's natural perfection now stands unveiled because all things have "put their evil nature off" (III. iv. 77).

VI

The image of the volcano and its analogues is especially prevalent throughout the final act, which is an exuberant celebration of the new age. Here, however, the image serves not as a pattern of dramatic action but as a symbol expressing the new cosmic joy and generative love that not only erupt with revolutionary tremors but also exhale a benign atmosphere which wraps and carries the world that has breathed it. From Demogor-

gon's dark cave beyond being, love explodes like an
earthquake to shake the mind-world to energy and form:
"like a storm bursting its cloudy prison / With thunder,
and with whirlwind," love

> has arisen
> Out of the lampless caves of unimagined being:
> With earthquake shock and swiftness making shiver
> Thought's stagnant chaos. . . .
>
> (IV. 376–80)

But the volcanic exhalation from the Power also embraces the world with an ambient atmosphere of joy and
love, so that Earth can tell of

> The joy, the triumph, the delight, the madness!
> The boundless, overflowing, bursting gladness,
> The vaporous exultation [48] not to be confined!
> Ha! ha! the animation of delight
> Which wraps me, like an atmosphere of light,
> And bears me as a cloud is borne by its own wind.[49]
>
> (IV. 319–24)

And the Moon, released from her prison of ice, experiences a similar self-enveloping exhalation of generative
love:

[48] Like the word "emotion" (see n. 26 above), this richly plays upon
its etymological meaning (to spring up vigorously) so as to remove all
distinction between mind and world, subject and object, and to embody
Shelley's thesis "that when speaking of the objects of thought, we
indeed only describe one of the forms of thought—or that, speaking
of thought, we only apprehend one of the operations of the universal
system of beings." See also IV. 333: "sound-exulting fountains."
[49] Shelley perhaps conceived of the cloud as moved by the wind that it
breathes out. Compare *Revolt of Islam,* IV. xxxi. 6: "On outspread
wings of its own wind upborne"; also *ibid.,* II. xxxi. 2–3.
  In the Moon's reply to Earth the line "Some Spirit is darted like a
beam from thee" (IV. 327) reads in the *Mask of Anarchy* MS: "Some
spirit wraps thine atmosphere and thee."

[183]

> A spirit from my heart bursts forth,
> It clothes with unexpected birth
> My cold bare bosom. . . .
>
> (IV. 359–61)

In the same manner that the purging volcanic ascent of Demogorgon made ridiculous, by contrast, the cruel lightning Jupiter flung down from heaven, the Earth can now mock the withdrawn Jupiter:

> Sceptred curse,
> Who all our green and azure universe
> Threatenedst to muffle round with black destruction,
> sending
> A solid cloud to rain hot thunderstones,

until all things "Were stamped by thy strong hate into a lifeless mire" (IV. 338–41, 349). This image of muffling, which defines the symbolic atmospheric condition imposed from without by a supposedly transcendent power, is opposed to the metaphor of clothing, wrapping, or enfolding that defines the spiritual atmosphere exhaled from within. For, Jupiter having been removed and "Heaven's despotism" having sunk into the "void abysm" (IV. 554–55), Earth can now breathe up a volcanic thunder of laughter and hear its echoes rebound not only from ocean and desert but also, and more importantly, from the now-vacant sky:

> Ha! ha! the caverns of my hollow mountains,
> My cloven fire-crags, sound-exulting fountains
> Laugh with a vast and inextinguishable laughter.
> The oceans, and the deserts, and the abysses,
> And the deep air's unmeasured wildernesses,
> Answer from all their clouds and billows, echoing after.[50]
>
> (IV. 332–37)

[50] Between the second and third of these lines, Huntington MS 2176, fol. 20ʳ, reads: "mouth of my ⟨volcanoes⟩." Over the canceled "volcanoes" Shelley added, "fire hills."

The spirit that informs this breath and fills the vacuum left in heaven by the removal of Jupiter's hate is love; and, like all active forces, it is an exhalation that rises from the earth's core and makes its way upward through the granite, roots, clay, leaves, and flowers until it spreads upon winds and clouds to form the atmosphere embracing that from whose heart it sprang. It makes the past a vital influence upon the present, just as the winter corpse exhales itself in spring flowers, for the same power that generates thought also causes the life of nature:

> It wakes a life in the forgotten dead,
> They breathe a spirit up from their obscurest bowers.
>
> (IV. 374–75)

In brief, as Demogorgon explains, shifting to an analogue of the volcano metaphor, Love "from its awful throne of patient power / . . . springs / And folds over the world its healing wings" (IV. 557, 560–61); and this throne of power, so like the one from which he himself has sprung to overcome Jupiter, he locates within, in "the wise heart" (IV. 588).

The symbolic significance of the effluence from within that becomes the enfolding atmosphere is, of course, that it expresses Shelley's rebellion against all extraneous impositions upon the mind and embodies in cosmic images his doctrine that perfectibility results from the mind's free admission of the indwelling Power. In addition to the many instances already mentioned, this symbolic design had been implicit in Act III in Earth's description of Prometheus' cave, where there are "bright golden globes / Of fruit, suspended in their own green heaven" (III. iii. 139–40). It accounts for the perfected Earth's likening himself, spinning "beneath my pyramid of night, / Which points into the heavens," to

> a youth lulled in love-dreams . . .
> Under the shadow of his beauty lying,
> Which round his rest a watch of light and warmth doth
> keep.[51]
>
> (IV. 444–49)

And the Moon informs the renovated Earth:

> Thou art folded, thou art lying
> In the light which is undying
> Of thine own joy, and heaven's smile divine.
>
> (IV. 437–39)

However, as these last lines intimate by picturing the perfected earth as wrapped not only in its own joyous light but also in the "smile" (light) of heaven, the symbol of the self-enveloping atmospheric exhalation is not quite adequate to Shelley's total theme. For his ethical doctrine also calls for some model of perfection, some image of the moral absolute, and in itself that meteorological symbol does not provide for it. It is noticeable that in nearly every instance the perfect exhaled atmosphere is likened to an irradiation of light, and evil is likened to an eclipsing darkness or veil. The veil image admirably suits Shelley's purpose because, like the evils rained down by Jupiter or the black destruction with

---

[51] This simile, which many readers have found confusing, rests upon Shelley's frequent identification of the human self as a world. The simile must be read as equating the dark pyramid, or cone, of Earth's night with the shadow of the youth's beauty, not his beauty itself, which is likened to the Earth's sunlight. Just as Earth sleeps within the conical shadow it casts by turning from the sun, so the youth lies within the shadow cast by his turning, through sleep, from his own beauty. That is, the sunlit heaven surrounding the pyramid of Earth's darkness is likened to the youth's beauty, which "round" (about, outside) his dark pyramid of sleep continues to give "light and warmth." When he is awake, his beauty is his own undimmed sunlit heaven; in sleep he lies under its tentlike shadow.

Compare *Witch of Atlas*, 60–61; ". . . she lay enfolden / In the warm shadow of her loveliness."

which he would muffle the earth, it implies a dark distortion superimposed on reality. Perfection is not an acquisition from without or a gift from above, and evil is not an inherent condition, but a mask. Perfection reveals itself when falsehood is removed from the truth it conceals and when, like the removal of Jupiter from heaven, "veil by veil, evil and error fall" (III. iii. 62) and all "such foul masks" are removed "with which ill thoughts / Hide that fair being" called man (III. iv. 44–45). Evil is like a low-lying mist that can be dissipated in the clearing air:

> Those ugly human shapes and visages
> . . . .
> Passed floating thro' the air, and fading still
> Into the winds that scattered them; and those
> From whom they passed seemed mild and lovely forms
> After some foul disguise had fallen. . . .
> . . . .
> All things had put their evil nature off.[52]
>
> (III. iv. 65–77)

Just as Jupiter is a phantomlike mockery of Prometheus, what man had called "life" before the new Promethean day was but a "painted veil . . . / Which mimicked, as with colours idly spread, / All men believed or hoped"; now it has been "torn aside"—"The loathsome mask has fallen, the man remains . . ." (III. iv. 190–93). Even what mortal man calls "life" is really a "veil" of death, since it is the existence of but a portion of the One Mind under the unreal conditions of mutability; and what man calls "death" is that sleep in which the unreal veil is removed from true life. Consequently, all that is unreal and evil is an eclipsing darkness that cuts the world off

[52] After this line in the draft Shelley wrote and then deleted, "Like an old garment soiled & overworn."

from light, and the result of the seismic eruption of Love is to shake thought's stagnant chaos "Till hate, and fear, and pain, light-vanquishing shadows, fleeing, / Leave Man . . . a sea reflecting love" (IV. 381–84).

The meteorological function of the irradiation of love's light from a cosmic center to form an enfolding atmosphere is therefore to cleanse that atmosphere of the illusory darkness of evil and error until it is transparent. For Shelley's ultimate image of the perfect condition is not merely that of Love springing up from its throne of power and folding over the world its healing wings. Rather, as a consequence of the world's exhaling its own radiant, darkness-withdrawing atmosphere of healing, perfection is the condition in which man and the world perfectly resemble or mirror the heaven. Earth must reflect the perfection the mind aspires to, not be darkened by a tyrannical fiction that it fears as a real being. The symbolism of the heaven-reflecting earth is recurrent in Shelley's poetry and frequently controls his poetic structures. Because *Adonais,* unlike *Prometheus Unbound,* is concerned with the immortality of the human soul and assumes a transcendent One which is Truth-Beauty-Goodness, this transfer of the thematic center of gravity from beneath to above curiously inverts the cosmic metaphor. Instead of the soul's radiating a light that clears the atmosphere so that heaven may be reflected in the soul, the transcendent One, represented as the sun, glows more brightly as the earthly soul more perfectly mirrors it and, by thus burning more intensely, evaporates the intervening clouds of mortal bondage:

> That Light whose smile kindles the Universe,
> That Beauty in which all things work and move,
> That Benediction which the eclipsing Curse
> Of birth can quench not, that sustaining Love

> Which through the web of being blindly wove
> By man and beast and earth and air and sea,
> Burns bright or dim, as each are mirrors of
> The fire for which all thirst; now beams on me,
> Consuming the last clouds of cold mortality.
>
> (478–86)

But when, as in *The Sensitive Plant,* Shelley's theme is the relative perfection of mortal life, rather than the absolute postmortal perfection, his basic image is of an earth that can mirror the starry skies, so that the starry flowers of the Venus-Lady's world-garden,

> the meteors of that sublunar Heaven,
> Like the lamps of the air when Night walks forth,
> Laughed round her footsteps up from the Earth!
>
> (II. 10–12)

This is also the heaven-earth relationship implicit in Shelley's complaint in his *Ode to Liberty* that words can "make the thoughts obscure / From which they spring," for then they are like lake-born clouds that "blot Heaven's blue portraiture" that should be painted in the mirroring lake. Mind alone is the source of those exhalations that intervene and prevent it from mirroring a heavenly perfection.

Thus in *Prometheus Unbound* when the Hour released above the earth the "prophecy" in Proteus' shell, the consequence was that the atmosphere, through an event like the transfiguration of Asia and Prometheus, became transparent:

> the impalpable thin air
> And the all-circling sunlight were transformed,
> As if the sense of love dissolved in them
> Had folded itself round the sphered world.
> My vision then grew clear, and I could see
> Into the mysteries of the universe.   (III. iv. 100–5)

This heaven to be reflected, unlike Jupiter's heaven, is not constituted by any hypothetical transcendent deity bent upon imposing himself on man. Unlike the Christian heaven, it does not assume the inherent depravity of man, the necessity of punishments and rewards, or the existence of a supreme ruler. On the contrary, like the One Mind, which contains in perfection all possible human minds, Shelley's heaven is symbolic of the absolute perfection that mind is able to conceive and become. It exists because mind is able to conceive and aspire to it, not because a deity creates and occupies it or because it has any existence apart from mind. Hence in her song of spiritual perfection at the end of Act II Asia can tell of being led by Prometheus to more-than-mortal realms "where the air we breathe is love" and where this air of love, by moving in the winds and on the waves, harmonizes "this earth with what we feel above" (II. v. 95–97). The heaven of perfection exists because it is felt to be, and the end of Shelley's symbolism is such translucence of the exhaled embracing atmosphere of love and light that the earth harmonizes with, or perfectly reflects, or is precisely analogous to, the heaven felt to be by the mind. Now that heaven is "free," it "rains fresh light and dew / On the wide earth," and earth is made "like heaven" (III. iv. 154–55, 160).

How mind constitutes this heaven, as opposed to the divinity-created heaven of the theologians, is made clear in Act IV. After their mystic dance with the Hours, the Spirits of the Human Mind divide into two groups, one to remain within the sphere enfolded by the earth's atmosphere, the other to soar beyond that envelope. There the second group will build "a new earth and sea, / And a heaven where yet [53] heaven could never be" (IV. 164–65) so long as there was a merely putative heaven

[53] Bodleian MS Shelley adds. e.12, fol. 101, reads, "till now."

inhabited by Jupiter, the supervisory and punitive deity. It is not St. John's God of the Apocalypse who will create a new heaven and a new earth for man; these lines in Shelley's final act echo ironically those in the final book of Scripture, for only the spirits of the human mind can build a heaven which is a model of perfection. Taking their plan not from some deity's purpose or idea but from the now-liberated world of man himself, they will build as an ideal the absolute, or Promethean, "world for the Spirit of Wisdom to wield" (IV. 155); and beneath this ideal of the mind all that belongs to earth will assemble to mirror it (IV. 152). In this sense, the mind's vision of the full perfection of its nature and the mind's actual mortal state—"heaven and earth"—are "united now" (IV. 273).

Throughout the play this symbolic relationship between heaven and earth recurrently draws various images into patterns that bind the earthly to the transcendent. It explains, for example, why it is inadequate to describe the perfected Earth merely as wrapped in the joyous light that it itself radiates and why Shelley felt the need to add, "and heaven's smile divine" (IV. 437–39). And it makes clear why, after describing the physicospiritual spring of the new age as descending from the winds of heaven, the poet balances this image by likening the spring to an atmospheric exhalation, a "joy which riseth up / As from the earth, clothing with golden clouds / The desert of our life" (II. i. 10–12). Somewhat more importantly, it accounts for Shelley's picture of the poet as one who

> will watch from dawn to gloom
> The lake-reflected sun illume
> The yellow bees in the ivy-bloom,
> Nor heed nor see, what things they be;
> But from these create he can

Forms more real than living man,
Nurslings of immortality!

(I. 743–48)

For the poet's concern is not things as things: having
access to a world so unencumbered by ugliness, error,
and evil that it is able to mirror the absolute perfection
that the mind can conceive for itself, he uses as the elements of his poetic shapings those images thus indirectly
illuminated by the mirroring world to which he is confined. But even though this accounts for the stuff of
poetic creation, the passage throws its emphasis not
upon those elements which the poet is constrained to
use, but upon his attention to the earth's act of illuminat-
ing and transforming its component things through its
capacity to resemble and thus to reflect the heavenly
light. For the imperfect mirror symbolizes the distortion
of unitary perfection into multiple hideous forms of falsehood and evil, just as Jupiter is the disfigured reflection
of Prometheus. Hence at the end of the play Earth will
plead that hate, fear, and pain flee like "light-vanquished
shadows" [54] so as to leave man, the microcosm,

who was a many-sided mirror,
Which could distort to many a shape of error
This true fair world of things, a sea reflecting love;
Which [55] over all his kind, as the sun's heaven
Gliding o'er ocean, smooth, serene, and even,
Darting from starry depths radiance and life, doth
move.[56]

(IV. 382–87)

[54] Bodleian MS Shelley adds. e. 12, fol. 54, reads, "like ⟨wind-⟩ light-
vanquished ⟨vapours⟩ shadows."
[55] I take "love" to be the antecedent of "Which."
[56] Contrast the Jehovah-like picture of Jupiter in Prometheus' curse,
"Let thy malignant spirit move / In darkness over those I love" (I.
276–77), which mocks Genesis 1:2: "and darkness was upon the face
of the deep. And the spirit of God moved upon the face of the waters."

[192]

As these passages intimate, then, the mortal condition closest to the ideal is that in which mutable human reality approximates, within its inherent limitations, the immutable, ideal perfection conceived by the mind; and the central cosmic symbol of this condition is the sea, constantly changing and yet free to reflect the changeless sky: "The Sea, in storm or calm, / Heaven's everchanging Shadow" (I. 27–28). This basic symbolic relationship Shelley elaborated into various image patterns, and the matrix from which they derive goes far toward explaining some of the metaphoric manner of his poem. When, for example, the Spirit of Earth describes the earthly perfection he has seen come into existence, he tells of two halcyons, birds whose domain is both sky and water, no longer carnivorous but feeding on nightshade, which is no longer poisonous: "and in the deep there lay / Those lovely forms imaged as in a sky" (III. iv. 82–83). In the last act, heaven and earth having been "united," the Spirits of the Human Mind explain that the human mind is the clear reflector of its own transcendent ideal. Once "dusk, and obscene, and blind," but now no longer shrouded in darkness, it is both "an ocean / Of clear emotion" and "A heaven of serene and mighty motion" (IV. 95–98); and consequently in its doubleness it is like the Spirits of the Human Mind, who divide into two groups, one to fashion, "beyond heaven," the ideal, the other to perform a parallel work in the "world of perfect light" (IV. 168).

Translated into myth, these cosmic symbols of heaven and the reflecting sea become the sun-god Apollo and Ocean, respectively, and constitute the grounds for Scene 2 of the third act. For it is fitting, in view of the nature of the symbolism, that the withdrawal of eclipsing Jupiter from the heavens be reported by the sun-god to Ocean, father of the Oceanids and, according to Aeschylus, Prometheus' sympathizer, and that the setting of this dialogue between heaven and the mirroring sea be Atlantis, not merely because Plato assigned it to the sea-god Poseidon, but also because in that earthly paradise he placed the ideal commonwealth of man.[57] In effect, heaven has communicated to earth the fact that the false barrier between them has been removed; and since Ocean's domain is the "Heaven-reflecting sea" (III. ii. 18), his prophecy of the coming perfection takes the form of an elaborate parallelism of sea and sky:

> Blue Proteus and his humid nymphs shall mark
> The shadow of fair ships, as mortals see
> The floating bark of the light-laden moon
> With that white star, its sightless pilot's crest,
> Borne down the rapid sunset's ebbing sea.
>
> (III. ii. 24–28)

[57] *Critias* 120.

CHAPTER V

⊰ THE FAR GOAL OF TIME ⊱

Up to this point the analysis of the drama has been based on the premise that Prometheus is the personification of Shelley's concept of the One Mind, but some qualification is now required. If, at the beginning of the play, Prometheus were truly the One Mind as Shelley defined that term, it would follow that he could not be represented by language. Imagery would falsify, not because Prometheus belongs to the imageless realm of Demogorgon outside sensible being, but because the supposed discreteness and diversity which we call "things" exist only in the human mind as a consequence of its necessary impurity. To adapt Demogorgon's words, unity is also imageless; and the One Mind is identical with the ineffable oneness of being. Even more important, were Prometheus precisely as he has here been defined, the narrative of the drama would have been impossible because the illusions of time, space, and change operate only in human minds. As the One Mind, Prometheus could have no history. The drama, then, can have been made possible only by the introduction of those unreal dimensions; and their introduction assumes that the One Mind can be less than its absolute nature

—indeed, must be, if human minds, its temporal portions, are distorted by evil. The absolute unity of being enters into time when it allows itself to be less than its own perfection, for time is merely the variable relationships made possible by the fracturing of unity into diversity. As Asia explains, it is not a reality but only the envious shadow cast by the throne of Saturn, Jupiter's predecessor and god of a vapid, mindless Golden Age (II. iv. 33–34). Saturn is Father Time only in the sense that the shadow he cast is the illusion of passing time. Permitted evil has compelled the One Mind into approximately the same illusory time-space, subject-object world that the human mind supposes. Only after his reunion with Asia and their withdrawal to the cave can Prometheus say of his existence,

> we will sit and talk of time and change,
> As the world ebbs and flows, ourselves unchanged.
> What can hide man from mutability?
>
> (III. iii. 23–25)

Although, as Prometheus' transfiguration revealed, the "form" that lives within him has been "unchanged" (II. i. 64–65), obviously what invests that form has undergone a history of change, just as Christ, the incarnation of the immutable Godhead, entered into mutable human circumstances. Nor has Shelley committed the contradiction of subjecting to change that which is declared to be unchangeable: Prometheus prophesies only that, despite man's necessary mutability, he himself will be outside time and change, not that it is a contradiction of his nature to re-enter them.

Consequently, upon Prometheus' entrance into his cave with Asia the possibility of narrative has ended, and he has passed beyond the limits of imagery and language. Only now is he truly the One Mind, and therefore he must disappear from the play. The final act is set near the cave of Prometheus, but neither Prometheus nor Asia reappears after their approach to the cave at the end of Act III. Even the drama's frame of reference has changed, for whereas the first three acts are Prometheus' story, in all of Act IV the observer's attention is directed instead to the spectacle of the human and cosmic analogues of the One Mind's perfection—the dances of the Hours and Spirits of the Human Mind and of the Spirits of the Earth and Moon. Because Asia and Prometheus have passed into an ineffable state, the final act is not really part of the Promethean drama but is a commentary on it conducted on the human plane. Indeed, although Mary Shelley described the last act as "a sort of hymn of rejoicing in the fulfilment of the prophecies with regard to Prometheus," it should more properly be thought of as belonging to the genre of the Jonsonian wedding masque, celebrating, as it does, the reunion of Prometheus and Asia that resolves the first three acts. Like such a masque, it is constituted of symbolic choral dances and joyous songs and ends with Demogorgon's speech of advice to the assembled elements that sums up the whole moral achievement of the action.

Only the imperfect Prometheus, then, can have been in time, but his task in time has been to bear the torch of hope to "this far goal of Time" (III. iii. 174). The goal of time for Prometheus, it is clear, is the end of time, the end of a fiction born of error and imperfection; and so it is for man when, having crossed the "night of life," he enters the grave. But the far goal of time on earth must be something else to man, who cannot be hidden from the dimensions of mutability. However perfected he has become, man is

> Nor yet exempt, though ruling them like slaves,
> From chance, and death, and mutability,
> The clogs of that which else might oversoar
> The loftiest star of unascended heaven,
> Pinnacled dim in the intense inane.   (III. iv. 200–4)

"Nor yet"; for when he will become entirely free of change he will no longer be man, the modified portion of the One Mind, but will be absorbed into the unity of being, just as Adonais is absorbed into the perfect One. However, if he can now make mutability his slave, his relation to time has been altered, although not severed. The two goals of time, then, do not result from any confusion by Shelley of a millennium with an apocalypse: [1] man, as man, can never transcend those relationships among thoughts called time, however much he may transform and subdue them. Shelley's apocalypse and millennium are the forms of perfection at the two different levels of being: the timelessness of the One Mind and the nearest possible approximation to that condition in the human mind, which subsists as human mind by virtue of the illusions of diversity and change.

The relation of these two goals of time is represented symbolically by the Spirit of the Hour who introduces the new age, the mind's analogue to nature's spring season, with which the Hora is traditionally identified. After bearing Asia to Prometheus so that they may withdraw into the immediate perfection of their timeless eternity, she is ordered then, but only then, to bring about the corollary event, the gradual perfecting of man within time. Thereafter, the Spirit of the Hour will not fade away like other Hours that have passed but will dwell beside the cave of Prometheus (III. iii. 83) because her

---

[1] This supposed confusion is one of the main concerns of Milton Wilson's *Shelley's Later Poetry.*

[198]

perfection will attend the One Mind timelessly. But meanwhile, after her earthly task has been performed and she has spread among mankind the prophecy contained in the shell, she interrupts her report of the gradual earthly purification she has observed to foretell how the instruments of her former temporal office will be made eternal. Since the classical Horae were assigned the task of yoking the horses of the sun each morning for its flight,[2] it is appropriate to the details of the conventional myth that the Hour's coursers, the temporal agents of her flight, should return on the completion of their task to their "birthplace in the sun" (III. iv. 108), which measures the passing of time. There, "Pasturing flowers of vegetable fire" (III. iv. 110),[3] they will be exempt from labor, never again to be the agents of passing time. Moreover, the Hour foresees, in a temple on the sun [4] will be installed her "moonlike" chariot [5] and statues of her Apollonian steeds imitating the "flight from which they find repose"—frozen, that is, in their

[2] Ovid *Metamorphoses* ii. 116–21; Lucian *Dialogues of the Gods* x. 1. Hyginus catalogues the names of the Horae and of the horses of the sun in the same fable (No. 183).

[3] In his account of Demogorgon, Boccaccio quoted Claudian's description of Eternity (see below, n. 29). Directly after the verses quoted by Boccaccio, Claudian had written of the return of the sun-god after he had elected to draw the Golden Age from among the four Ages secreted in Eternity's cave: the sun-god then "entered his garden which dripped dew of golden fires, his vale surrounded by a flaming stream that pours radiant light into the plants on which the horses of the Sun pasture (*quae Solis pascuntur equi*). Here he gathers flowers with which he decks the heads, the golden reins, and manes of his horses" (*De consulatu Stilichonis* ii. 467–72). Shelley had quoted Claudian's *Carmen paschale* (as his *De salvatore* was formerly entitled) in a note to *Queen Mab*.

[4] Rather like the temple of Apollo described by Ovid (*Metamorphoses* ii. 1ff.), but even more like the temple of the sun at Heliopolis as described by Strabo (*Geography* xvii. 1, 28).

[5] For the representations of the Horae as charioteers, see George M. A. Hanfmann, *The Season Sarcophagus in Dumbarton Oaks* (Cambridge, Mass., 1951), I, 159–63.

motion—and these two symbols of the temporal succession of sun and moon, day and night, will be yoked by an "amphisbaenic snake." Now, the serpent serves elsewhere in the poem as emblematic of a mode of time, and Shelley's peculiar choice here of the serpent with a head at each end and his use of it as the means of joining emblems of sun and moon require that it also be interpreted in terms of time. Joining the two poles of diurnal movement and notable for its ability to move in either direction, the amphisbaenic snake, by tautly arresting two opposing motions, serves as a kind of zodiacal sign of the dynamic capture of the perfect present. Time is obviously not at an end for man: like eternal spring, the symbol of the perfect present brought by the vernal Hour will persist on the sun, which continues to measure out time.[6] Yet its persistence will not be inert or inevitable, for the serpent represents a tension and threatens to move in either direction. There are, then, at least two different conceptions of eternity in the poem, and they are not to be confused. The symbols of the Hour's temporal role are to be fixed in the moving sun, but she herself is to attend the cave of Prometheus and Asia: presiding over the human mind will be a continuing duration of the arrested present, a kind of *nunc stans,* but from the One Mind the illusion of time has dropped out entirely.

Corresponding to these two forms of eternity, Prometheus and Asia disappear into the cave and vanish from the drama, and the masque-like final act is set in the adjacent forest, the *sylva* of the human world. In other

---

[6] Compare *Queen Mab,* VIII. 53–57:

> O human Spirit! spur thee to the goal
> Where virtue fixes universal peace,
> And midst the ebb and flow of human things,
> Show somewhat stable, somewhat certain still,
> A lighthouse o'er the wild of dreary waves.

words, the frame of reference of the drama has shifted radically from the One Mind of the first three acts to the purified human world, where we now view the cosmic symbols of the new Promethean age of man, the most comprehensive temporal approximations to the atemporal state of Prometheus. Each of the two cosmic dances of the masque effects a union and interpenetration celebrating and paralleling those of Prometheus and Asia; and the relation of the first set of dancers, the Hours and Spirits of the Human Mind, to the second set, the Spirits of Earth and Moon, may be recognized as the relation of the "subjective" mind to the "objective" universe. The two dances celebrate the perfection of the two worlds into which man supposes reality to be divided. The whirling dance of the Spirits of Earth and Moon is, of course, a representation of the harmonious motions of all the heavenly bodies, of which human dance, according to tradition, was an imitation. Plato had likened the movement of the stars to a dance because they meet with each other and yet keep and repeat their own orbits; [7] and, to choose one of Shelley's favorite authors, Jonson ended his *Masque of Beauty* with a song exhorting the dancers,

> Still turn and imitate the heaven
> In motion swift and even;
> And as his planets go,
> Your brighter lights do so.

Lucian, another of Shelley's favorites, not only traced human dance back to the cosmic dance but also associated it with the ancient mysteries:

Historians . . . tell you that Dance came into being contemporaneously with the primal origin of the universe,

[7] *Timaeus* 40c.

making her appearance together with Love—the love that is age-old. In fact, the concord of the heavenly spheres, the interlacing of the errant planets with the fixed stars, their rhythmic agreement and timed harmony, are proofs that Dance was primordial . . . not a single ancient mystery-cult can be found that is without dancing, since they were established, of course, by Orpheus and Musaeus, the best dancers of that time, who included it in their prescriptions as something exceptionally beautiful to be initiated with rhythm and dancing.[8]

The dance that Shelley called "the mystic measure" (IV. 129) and that Milton called the "Mystical dance" of the heavenly bodies [9] is not merely exemplary of perfect order but expresses the divine harmony. Spiritual rather than physical, it is the work of love, not of astronomical laws.[10]

But the Dance of the Hours is also a recognizable commonplace, and Shelley's usual mythopoeic processes might well lead us to suspect that, in addition to the simple design of the "subjective" and "objective" harmonies expressed by the two dances, he is complicating the texture of Act IV by transforming and assimilating mythic patterns in his presentation of the first dance. The Horae, or Hours, were generally understood as the deities of the various seasons, and their circular dance represented the harmoniously periodic movement of time. All the Horae were traditionally the attendants of Venus, but the name was associated especially with the

---

[8] *De saltatione* 7, 15. For a brief account of the tradition of the cosmic dance, see John C. Meagher, "The Dance and the Masques of Ben Jonson," *Journal of the Warburg and Courtauld Institutes*, XXV (1962), 258–77.

[9] *Paradise Lost*, V. 619–27.

[10] See also Richard Payne Knight, "The Mystic Dance," in *Symbolic Language of Ancient Art and Mythology* (New York, 1876 [1st ed., 1818]).

spring, Venus' season, and was frequently used as a synonym for it in Greek. Since it was the spring Hora that, according to the myth, received the goddess when she floated ashore on a shell after her sea-birth, Shelley was consistent with the spirit and general design of the myth in calling upon the vernal Hour to conduct Asia to Prometheus in a shell-like chariot upon her spiritual rebirth, which is explicitly made analogous to her original birth out of the sea. It is further appropriate that the same Hour, thus identified with Asia and the reborn spirit of love and life, surround the earth with the new Promethean spring by releasing it from the shell given to Asia by Proteus and that she then, as an eternal spring, forever attend Prometheus and Asia as her mythic prototype attended Venus.

But Venus was also traditionally accompanied by another group, sometimes considered her daughters; these, the Charites, or Graces, were understood to express the benevolent, joyous powers surrounding the goddess' character and, like the Hours, were regularly associated with spring and represented in circular dance. As a consequence of these similarities, the Hours and Graces, each usually three in number, were very often joined in mythology and occasionally even confused with each other. Both groups, moreover, were understood as personifications of particular virtues and delights, the Hours being identified as Irene, Dike, and Eunomia (Peace, Justice, and Law, or Order) and the Graces as Aglaia, Euphrosyne, and Thalia (Splendor, Joy, and Flourishing). Perhaps Banier best captured the general conception of the Graces when he interpreted them as "the Charms of the Mind," adding:

Among the many Divinities invented by the Ancients, none were more amiable than the *Graces*, since it was from them the Rest borrowed their Charms, Sources of every Thing agreeable and smiling in Nature. They gave to Places, Persons, Works, and to every thing in its kind, that finished Charm which crowns all its other Perfections, and is as it were the Flower of its Excellence.[11]

The very name, Graces,—that is, favors, or benefits—reveals that these deities were thought to have as their special duty the conferring of benefits on man: they "on men all gracious gifts bestow, / Which deck the body or adorn the mind." [12] But invariably the Horae, Venus' other attendants, were also described as pre-eminently beneficent, for they

> open-handed sit upon the clouds,
> And press the liberality of heaven
> Down to the laps of thankfull men.[13]

The kind of embracing cosmic harmony and universal perfection that the commingled Hours and Graces consequently tended to symbolize can be judged by a passage in Proclus' commentary on Plato's *Timaeus* in which Proclus pictures a Grace and an Hour combining their beneficent moral forces to give perfect order to each of the celestial spheres: [14]

[11] Abbé Banier, *The Mythology and Fables of the Ancients*, II, 351, 348. Pindar (*Olympian* xiv. 5–6) wrote that by the aid of the Graces all things pleasant are brought about for mortals; in *An Inscription for a Temple Dedicated to the Graces* Samuel Rogers elaborated on this theme:

> From them flow all the decencies of Life;
> Without them nothing pleases, Virtue's self
> Admired not loved: and those on whom They smile,
> Great though they be, and wise, and beautiful,
> Shine forth with double lustre.

[12] Spenser, *Faerie Queene*, VI. x. 23. See also Seneca's discussion of the Graces in his *De beneficiis;* and Banier, *The Mythology and Fables of the Ancients*, II, 353.

[13] Jonson, *New Inn*, I. vi. 141–43. See also the *Homeric Hymn to Apollo* 194.

[14] I quote Thomas Taylor's translation in his edition of Pausanias' *Description of Greece* ([2d ed.; London, 1824], III, 315–16), because Shelley ordered this work in 1817.

Theologists place *Eunomia* over the inerratic sphere, who separates the multitude which it contains, and perpetually preserves every thing in its proper order: and hence celebrating *Vulcan* as the fabricator of the heavens, they conjoin him with *Aglaia*, because she gives splendour to every part of the heavens, through the variety of the stars. And again, they place *Justice*, one of the seasons, over the planetary spheres; because this deity gives assistance to the inequality of their motions, and causes them through proportion to conspire into equality and consent: but of the Graces they conjoin with this divinity *Thalia*, because she gives perfection to the ever-flourishing lives which they contain. But they place *Peace* over the sublunary region, because this divinity appeases the war of the elements; but of the Graces they associate with this divinity *Euphrosyne* because she confers a facility of natural energy on each of the elements.

These are representative interpretations of the cluster of myths that Shelley has reconstituted to fashion the Hours and Spirits of the Human Mind of Act IV; and it should also be evident that the same Spirits who come from the human mind to console Prometheus in agony in Act I take their nature from these same notably beneficent Graces, personifications of the mind's powers, whom Shelley substituted there for the Christian God's ministering angel. Like the personified Graces, the spirits who comfort Prometheus can be recognized as Reform (or Revolution in its best sense, as the prelude to freedom and love), Self-Sacrifice, Wisdom, and Poetry; and just as the Graces are but the attendants of Venus, not Venus herself, so these spirits of the human mind, however fair, prove inadequate without the Love that Asia symbolizes. The mental Graces having exercised the limits of their power in Act I, the spring Hour appears in Acts II and III to transport Asia to Prometheus—as the Hora, after receiving the newly risen Aphrodite, led her to the palace of the gods [15]—and then to disseminate the new spiritual season. Now in the celebrative final act Shelley at last brings together the Hours and Spirits of the Human Mind to intermingle them in a symbolic masque-like dance. All the conventional similarities and interconnections of the Hours and Graces that have been mentioned are themselves a sufficient motive for Shelley's weaving together their two traditional dances. Yet this, too, is Shelley's adaptation of an established myth, for the *Homeric Hymn to Apollo* depicts a dance of the Graces and Hours, together with Aphrodite, Harmonia, and Hebe, each holding the other by the hand; Xenophon, a dance of the Graces, Hours, and Nymphs; and Apuleius, a dance of the Hours and Graces around the figure of Venus.[16] However, before we can properly examine the symbolism of Shelley's adaptation of the dance of the Hours and Graces, it will be necessary to return to his dramatization of the theme of time and eternity.

The final act opens with the funeral procession of the "past Hours" bearing "Time to his tomb in eternity" (IV. 31, 14). Since the pallbearers are the past Hours and since they are aware of the coming of new Hours, "children of a diviner day" (IV. 26), there is no reason for understanding this event to mean, as some critics have believed, that all of time is at an end. The frame of reference of this act, unlike the rest of the drama, is not the One Mind, but the time-bound human mind; and clearly Time, the "Father of many a cancelled year" (IV. 11) as distinct from the "diviner day" that fathers the new Hours, must be the order of temporality prior to the in-

---

[15] See the *Homeric Hymn to Aphrodite.*
[16] *Homeric Hymn to Apollo* 189–206; Xenophon *Symposium* vii. 5; Apuleius *Metamorphoses* x. 32.

stitution of the Promethean age. The necessary chain of events instituted by the reign of Jupiter has come to its end with his overthrow; hence the past years have been "cancelled," and the kind of time that is to be will differ from both past time and the timelessness of Prometheus. Since time is the perceived relationships among illusory diversities, the Time that is buried must have been constituted by the kind of relationships that subsisted while man's mind was shackled by tyranny and superstition and that thus caused time to be a swift succession of transient moments. What the Promethean order of human time is to be is suggested by the fact that when the new Hours first appear they are observed by Ione and Panthea to be charioteers like their predecessors, but, to Panthea's bewilderment, without chariots (IV. 56), for, paradoxically, they are the elements of moving time but without the means of rapid flight. They are the fondly delaying presence of that which by definition passes away. Some further sense of the kind of time Shelley is attempting to represent may be gained from an unused manuscript verse [17] which describes the new Hours as "chainless" and, unlike the past Hours, "kingless," [18] for the intimation is that the new time is not a linked succession or series of evanescent moments, each dragging the next into the past, but a kind of free republic of independent, coexisting units.

Because the dimensions of mutability are functions of the condition of the human mind, transient time must diminish as a factor of experience in proportion as the mind grows more nearly perfect. Even as early as *Queen Mab* Shelley had prophesied such progress of the human mind toward the fullness of its potentialities that Time,

---

[17] Bodleian MS Shelley adds. e.12, fol. 85.
[18] Compare IV. 20: "the corpse of the King of Hours!"

once the "conqueror" who had "ruled the world," would fall and flee.[19] Eventually the thoughts of ideally virtuous man will rise in "time-destroying infiniteness" and "gift" him

> With self-enshrined eternity, that mocks
> The unprevailing hoariness of age,
> And man, once fleeting o'er the transient scene
> Swift as an unremembered vision, stands
> Immortal upon earth.
>
> (*Queen Mab*, VIII. 203–11)

But this does not mean, any more than does the burial of Time in *Prometheus Unbound,* that time is at an end and that man will experience the timelessness of Prometheus. The same temporal term acquires quite different meanings when applied to the One Mind and when applied to the human mind. What Shelley meant by *human* "time," "eternity," and "time-destroying infiniteness" he tried to make clear in a Lockean commentary on the verses just quoted from the earlier poem:

Time is our consciousness of the succession of ideas in our mind. Vivid sensation, of either pain or pleasure, makes the time seem long, as the common phrase is, because it renders us more acutely conscious of our ideas. If a mind be conscious of a hundred ideas during one minute, by the clock, and of two hundred during another, the latter of these spaces would actually occupy so much greater extent in the mind as two exceed one in quantity. If, therefore, the human mind, by any future improvement of its sensibility, should become conscious of an infinite number of ideas in a minute, that minute would be eternity. I do not hence infer that the actual space between the birth and death of a man will ever be prolonged; but that his sensibility is perfectible, and that

---

[19] IX. 23–37.

the number of ideas which his mind is capable of receiving is indefinite. One man is stretched on the rack during twelve hours; another sleeps soundly in his bed: the difference of time perceived by these two persons is immense; one hardly will believe that half an hour has elapsed, the other could credit that centuries had flown during his agony. Thus, the life of a man of virtue and talent, who should die in his thirtieth year, is, with regard to his own feelings, longer than that of a miserably priest-ridden slave, who dreams out a century of dulness. The one has perpetually cultivated his mental faculties, has rendered himself master of his thoughts, can abstract and generalize amid the lethargy of every-day business; —the other can slumber over the brightest moments of his being, and is unable to remember the happiest hour of his life. Perhaps the perishing ephemeron enjoys a longer life than the tortoise.

That duration is subjective and is measured by consciousness is not, of course, Shelley's discovery, however consonant it is with the rest of his philosophic idealism, and one would have found the doctrine not only in Godwin's *Political Justice,* to which he refers in the note quoted, but also in Locke and all those he influenced, including Sterne and Condillac.[20] The Time that the past Hours bury, then, is not all of chronological time, but that temporal order in which moments flee in rapid succession because of the mind's imperfect consciousness; it is the time that rules the mind instead of being ruled by it, and therefore it has significant analogies with that other tyrannical fiction, Jupiter, and belongs to his reign. The new Hours of the diviner day constitute an eternity, not in the sense of Prometheus' timelessness nor in the sense of the persistence in time of the changeless present, symbolized by the statue of the Hour's horses

[20] *Oeuvres,* ed. Thèry, III, 308.

and chariot, but in the sense of the *indefinite* capacity of the human mind's awareness. For if the human mind is indefinitely perfectible and therefore capable of holding in a moment a quantity of ideas to which no number can be assigned, then the mental time constituted by the quantity of these ideas also becomes immeasurable, infinite. In human time "eternity" is a condition of the mind in which no fixed limits can be set on consciousness.[21]

Hence Shelley's interpretation and assimilation of that ideal pattern he found in the traditional interweaving dance of the Hours and Graces. Only absolute unity can be outside time, space, and mutability; but the world of mutability can tend toward that unity through the relational flowing together of its component diversities so as to overcome diversity, just as the human mind's potentiality of holding together an indeterminate number of discrete ideas is its mode of attaining an "eternity" in time. Dance, then, corresponds to the "order," "arrange-

[21] In the note quoted from *Queen Mab* Shelley refers the reader to Condorcet's *Esquisse d'un tableau historique des progrès de l'esprit humain*, and although Condorcet is prophesying a protraction of man's chronological life, he is helpful in clarifying Shelley's use of the word "indefinite": "Certainly man will not become immortal, but will not the interval between the first breath that he draws and the time when in the natural course of events, without disease or accident, he expires, increase indefinitely? . . . In truth, this average span of life which we suppose will increase indefinitely as time passes, may grow in conformity either with a law such that it continually approaches a limitless length but without ever reaching it, or with a law such that through the centuries it reaches a length greater than any determinate quantity that we may assign to it as its limit. In the latter case such an increase is truly indefinite in the strictest sense of the word, since there is no term on this side of which it must of necessity stop. In the former case it is equally indefinite in relation to us, if we cannot fix the limit it always approaches without ever reaching, and particularly if, knowing only that it will never stop, we are ignorant in which of the two senses the term 'indefinite' can be applied to it. Such is the present condition of our knowledge as far as the perfectibility of the human race is concerned; such is the sense in which we may call it indefinite" (*The Progress of the Human Mind*, trans. June Barraclough [London, 1955], p. 200).

ment," or "combination" of particulars that the poet effects under the compulsion of his extraordinary and ineffable apprehension of absolute unity; and the "web of the mystic measure" woven by the choral dance of the Hours and Spirits of the Human Mind (IV. 129) is the ideal rhythm unifying time and mental powers. The web is the interpenetration of the two so that "the Hours, and the spirits of might and pleasure, / Like the clouds and sunbeams, unite" (IV. 79–80) or chiastically intermingle "As the flying-fish leap / . . . And mix with the sea-birds half asleep" (IV. 86–88). This intertexture and interfusion of mind and time is the formation of purely mental time instead of the swiftly passing time resulting from the imperfect mind's illusion that time is an external reality. Since the most nearly perfect mental time possible is "eternal" because it has no limits, and not because it is either timelessness or the sum of time, it is represented as infinitely slow and thus as the temporal approximation of timelessness. During his torture Prometheus, being in time, had suffered its amplitude through the expanded consciousness of pain, so that the moments were "divided by keen pangs / Till they seemed years" (I. 13–14). But for the human mind in Jovian time day had passed with speed, and time lingered only in the "night of time" that symbolizes the meaningless empty spaces of human life:

> Once the hungry Hours were hounds
> Which chased the day like a bleeding deer,
> And it limped and stumbled with many wounds
> Through the nightly dells of the desert year.
> (IV. 73–76)

Now that the Hours and the virtuous powers of the mind are interpenetrated, the "day" of man's existence is pro-

tracted and his "night" overcome. Instead of hastening
the day into lengthened night, the new Hours that attend
the earth are

> Solemn and slow, and serene, and bright,
> Leading the Day and outspeeding the Night,
> With the powers of a world of perfect light.[22]
>
> (IV. 166–68)

For the effect of the interwoven dance and song of the
Hours and Spirits is to

> Enchant the day that too swiftly flees,
> To check its flight ere the cave of Night.
>
> (IV. 71–72)

Human time cannot stop altogether, but the powers of
the mind can now detain it indefinitely because of the
infinite expansion of consciousness. Lovers, for example,
catch the Hours in their woven caresses, and Wisdom,
the Siren, delays their ships of passage (IV. 105–10).[23]
The human mind rules time, its slave, and subdues it to
near-irrelevance.

Thus far we have observed that Shelley has provided
for three different kinds of eternity: the timelessness that
is, by definition, the condition of the One Mind, which
has nothing to do with the illusion of time; the unchang-
ing persistence of the ideal state during time; and the
boundlessness of mental duration in the free and perfectible human mind. Yet none of these categories ade-

---

[22] Only those Hours that are driven "beyond heaven" are "Ceaseless and
rapid" (IV. 163), but their speed is not that of transience; it is to hasten the construction of an ideal model for man by those Spirits of his
mind that transcend the limitations of human mutability, or that, unlike the thoughts confined to human existence, can "float above" its
"darkness," as Shelley expressed it in *Mont Blanc*.

[23] In Bodleian MS Shelley adds. e.12, fol. 88, after line 76, Shelley wrote:
"But now like a fawn it [the day] lingers & listens / In the net of music
whose meshes are air."

quately provides for Demogorgon's identification of himself as "Eternity" (III. i. 53), for his picture of an "Eternity" that may free the "serpent that would clasp her with his length" (IV. 565–67), or even for the fact that past Time is borne to his tomb in "eternity" (IV. 14). When in Act II Asia and Panthea were being drawn by Necessity into Demogorgon's cave, the Spirits inhabiting the physical world and symbolizing its dynamic forces sang of the perpetually repeated rise and fall of the nightingales' song as representative of the way in which Power manifests itself in the temporal course of natural events; and the Fauns that inhabit the world of matter then described a similar infinitely repeated cycle of natural events. For in the natural world the cloud, in unceasing repetition, dissolves in rain and is resurrected from its tomb; indeed,

> All things that move and breathe with toil and sound
> Are born and die; revolve, subside, and swell.[24]

Only in the imprisoned and enslaved human mind is time a linear chain of moments, each of which is dissipated as the next linked moment arises; to the liberated and amplified human mind an illimitable number of nonlinear moments are simultaneously available. In the natural world, which freely and passively admits the Power and its law of Necessity, time both passes and is preserved, for it is a perpetually repeated circle without beginning or end.

But the circle is also the shape that Shelley assigns to Eternity in accordance with the ubiquitous emblem tradition that depicts Eternity as a figure holding or, more often, surrounded by, a serpent bent into a circle, with its tail in its mouth, to represent the unendingness of

---

[24] *Mont Blanc*, 95–96.

time. Not only is this circular serpent the "doom"—that is, all the events destined to be—that clasps Eternity (IV. 567–69); it also appears as the "snake-like Doom coiled" underneath the throne of "the Eternal, the Immortal" in Demogorgon's region outside being (II. iii. 95–96). Whereas the amphisbaenic snake represents the retention of the perfect present during the course of moving time, the circular serpent, tail in mouth, is the emblem of the totality of time. Because mutability is the inherent condition of the natural world, eternity in that domain is the *moving* circle, the whole possible course of events perpetually renewing and repeating itself. This circular model of time helps explain why Asia paradoxically describes life's journey from cave to ocean as a passage from age, through infancy, and beyond an entrance-exit that is both "Death and Birth." Life is a circle that ends where it begins, not a line that abandons one point for another. The same temporal circle also gives full meaning to the otherwise strange refrain of the Spirits of the Human Mind that come to console Prometheus at the end of Act I: "we bear the prophecy / Which begins and ends in thee!" (I. 690–91, etc.). Beginning and end meet: the serpent bites its own tail. In terms of the doctrine of Necessity, "Similar circumstances produce the same unvariable effects" in both the physical and moral worlds, and hence Shelley's conception of prophecy: [25] because knowledge of cause is foreknowledge of consequence, one may behold in the present, "as in a glass, / The future" (I. 661–63).[26] Present contains future, and if there were no time at all, the two would be a single point; translated into sequen-

---

[25] Note to *Queen Mab*, on Necessity.
[26] Compare *Hellas*, 805–6: "The coming age is shadowed on the Past / As on a glass."

tial time, present and future are not opposite poles of a line, but the coinciding beginning and end of a circle. Consequently, while Prometheus is in time, his motive for perfection and the perfection that necessarily follows from that motive become one only in the course of the circular motion of time.[27]

However, Shelley's two references to the circular serpent of eternity locate it, not in Prometheus' realm, where eternity is the absence of time, nor in mankind's, where the models of eternity are the duration of the perfect present, the infinitude of mental awareness, and the perpetually repeated circle of the sum of time, but in Demogorgon's realm of Power, outside being. This emblematic serpent, moreover, is dormant, motionless, not the endlessly repeating circle of the sensible world, and thus it accords in its nature with the sleeping volcanic Demogorgon before he is awakened to action by Asia. Similarly, in *The Daemon of the World* Shelley had described the "vast snake Eternity" as ever lying in "charmed sleep" and had located it, too, behind the veil covering "nature's inner shrine."[28] Boccaccio had supplied Shelley with the myth that Demogorgon had Eternity[29] as his companion and was so fearsome that no

---

[27] Note to *Queen Mab*, on Necessity: "Motive is to voluntary action in the human mind what cause is to effect in the material universe." Compare Shelley to Leigh Hunt, 1 May 1820: "If faith is a virtue in any case[,] it is so in politics rather than religion; as having a power of producing that[,] a belief in which is at once a prophecy & a cause—."
[28] See also *Revolt of Islam*, IV. iv. 5–6.
[29] Like innumerable other mythographers, Boccaccio, quoting Claudian, also assigns to Eternity—whom he defines as the immeasurable totality of time—the emblem of the serpent devouring his own tail, "thus in his movement tracing his own beginning. . . . For the end of one year is always the beginning of the next and will be thus while time lasts." Eternity herself, Boccaccio adds, gives out the periods of time and also recalls them into her bosom, just as Shelley has past Time borne to his tomb in Eternity, withdrawn from actuality into potentiality, like everything else in time. Moreover, Boccaccio places Eternity in a cave which

one dared pronounce his name, and all this, in his usual myth-making manner, Shelley adapted to his own purposes; for when Jupiter asks Demogorgon to identify himself he replies, "Eternity. Demand no direr name" (III. i. 52). In the context of Shelley's play Demogorgon is entitled to the name "Eternity"—among his infinite other appropriate names—because as the Power, or absolute potentiality, he bears the relation to actuality that eternity bears to time. He is eternity because he is the infinitude of all the events that occur in time; but he also has "direr" names because, depending upon how Power is admitted by mind into actuality, potentiality can be released as a Jupiter or a revolution or any other disturbance. Correspondingly, the "snake-like Doom coiled underneath" the throne of "the Eternal, the Immortal"—it is unimportant whether or not we identify this figure with Demogorgon, since under any circumstances he must subsume it—is that totality of time which, self-enclosing and dormant, constitutes the last of Shelley's various conceptions of eternity. It is, for example, the "eternity," or sum total of time, in which we are told is located the tomb to which former Time has been borne by the past Hours, just as Jupiter is withdrawn from actuality to the infinite potentiality. Lying thus outside being, the sleeping, inert circle under Eternity's throne can be aroused and unloosed through "life's portal"; uncoiled, it enters being as sequential time and change. But on being released as moving time, its course is not random or arbitrary; the serpent of Eternity is the "Doom" in the sense of "destiny" because its determined course is inherent in it, in accordance with the law of Necessity. Like

is, he says, far off, unknown, and inaccessible (*impervia*) to the human mind and thus is like the unknowable, infinitely remote realm of Power in Shelley's philosophy.

Demogorgon, the serpent of Eternity is neither good nor
evil, and all discussions of the question in these terms are
beside the point: the coiled serpent is merely the morally
indifferent possibility of the entrance into the world of a
sequence of events. Consequently, it can, through that
"meekness" which is the willed submission of the human
spirit to the natural order of things, enter the world to
overthrow the unnatural Jovian regime; or, after the institution of the Promethean age, it can once again be released to introduce another sequence of temporal change.

It is supremely fitting that, as that Eternity which is
the totality of possible time, Demogorgon return to the
drama at its very end, like the final moral commentator
in the masque, to summon together his audience and
offer his lecture on the relation of potentiality to time.
The One Mind has now been released from time, the imperfection of being. For mankind, confined to mutable
being, the perfect moment has been arrested during the
continued movement of time; in the perfected human
mind, time, although still necessarily in flux, has become
illimitable; and in man's sensible world the totality of
time moves in its eternal circle of renewal. Finally, in
Demogorgon's cave—the unknowable realm of the ultimate cause of all that man experiences as actual—the
total potentiality of temporal change sleeps as a self-
enclosing serpent that Shelley has ironically substituted
for the serpent Satan, who is imprisoned by God's angel
in the bottomless pit at the end of the Christian Scripture. But, although Demogorgon's final speech mock-
ingly echoes the Book of Revelation (20:1–3), replacing
the Devil with mutability, Shelley has not promised an
apocalypse for man, and nothing in his handling of time
demands it; nor has he fatuously blinded himself to the
moral stress continuously imposed upon man to sustain

the highest perfection that belongs to his nature. It is inherent in the order of things that the potentiality of temporal change tend to become actual, that because of the inherent weakness of the potentiality of change to sustain itself as only potentiality,

> with infirm hand, Eternity,
> Mother of many acts and hours, should free
> The serpent that would clasp her with his length.
>
> (IV. 565–67)

Man is continuously subject to this threat; and Demogorgon, who, after all, is the ultimate authority on the relation of the possible to the actual, calls on man for the wholehearted exercise of "Gentleness, Virtue, Wisdom, and Endurance" as the means of reassuming an "empire o'er the disentangled doom" (IV. 569) and inhibiting the inherent compulsion toward a new order of events and time.

❦ INDEX ❧

A

Aeschylus: *Epigoni,* 80; *Eumenides,* 77; *Prometheus Bound,* 39, 40, 42, 46–47, 61, 67, 69, 77, 81, 82–88, 92, 97, 157–58, 194; *Prometheus the Torch-Bearer,* 75; *Seven Against Thebes,* 162
Alciati, Andrea, 116
Almond tree, 116–17
Anchises, 119–20, 122, 135–36, 138, 139
Aphrodite. *See* Venus
Apollo, 193
Apollodorus, 69, 159
Apuleius, 83, 206
Aristotle, 21
Atlantis, 194
Aurora, 65–66

B

Bacon, Francis, 124, 160, 179–80
Banier, Abbé, 77, 155, 173, 203–4
Berkeley, George, 5, 6, 7, 10, 12–13, 16, 18, 21, 26, 39, 49
Bible, 92–105, 145, 182, 191, 192, 217
Bladud, King, 66, 168

Boccaccio, 154–56, 159, 199, 215
Bradley, F. H., 13
Brucker, Jacob, 119
Burnet, Thomas, 42
Byron, 1

C

Cabanis, P.-J.-G., 41, 122
Chambers, A. B., 179
Chambers, Ephraim, 166, 168
Christ, 92, 93, 95–108, 196
Cicero, 20, 80
Cirillo, Albert R., 45
Claudian, 199, 215
Cleanthes (the Stoic), 80–81
Coleridge, S. T., 5, 7, 15, 154
Comes, Natalis, 160
Condorcet, Jean A., 210
Cupid, 73–74, 76

D

Dance, 201–3, 206, 210–12
Delphic oracle, 76–78, 141–42, 173
Diodorus Siculus, 76
Diogenes Laertius, 20, 81
Dionysius of Heraclea, 80–81

[219]

INDEX

INDEX

[221]

INDEX

Shelley, P. B. (*continued*)
anity, 30, 57, 179; *Future State,
A,* 13, 27, 29; *Hellas,* 11, 19, 22,
45, 95, 105, 214; *Hymn to In-
tellectual Beauty,* 57; *Julian and
Maddalo,* 35; *Laon and Cythna,*
36; *Lines Written among the
Euganean Hills,* 108; *Mask of
Anarchy,* 164; *Mont Blanc,* 4,
17, 23, 25, 27, 34, 113, 127,
130, 144, 146, 148–49, 151,
212, 213; *Necessity of Atheism,
The,* 8; *Ode to Liberty,* 35, 57,
70, 108, 113, 151, 152–53, 189;
On Life, 4, 10–13 *passim,* 49,
131–32, 152; *On Love,* 51, 136;
On Polytheism, 27; *On the
Devil and Devils,* 8, 10, 57, 126;
*Philosophical View of Reform,
A,* 107, 108, 109, 110; *Queen
Mab,* 4, 8, 9, 25, 29, 35, 41,
42, 71, 89, 126, 139, 149, 199,
200, 207–9, 210, 214, 215; *Re-
futation of Deism,* 9, 12, 28,
42; *Revolt of Islam,* 29, 33, 36,
71, 108, 127, 139, 141, 145,
150, 162, 163, 183, 215; *Rosa-
lind and Helen,* 72; *Sensitive
Plant, The,* 26, 59, 70, 71, 123,
146, 150, 189; *Speculations on
Metaphysics,* 4, 10–31 *passim,*
40, 49, 126; *Triumph of Life,*
179; *Vindication of Natural
Diet, A,* 41; *Witch of Atlas,* 186
Silenus, 118, 119, 123
Silius Italicus, 159–60, 164
Smith, Kirby Flower, 73
Sophocles, 74
Spenser, Edmund, 60–61, 204
Spinoza, 7
Spirit of the Earth. *See* Earth
Spirits of the Human Mind, 3,
32, 102, 104, 142, 171–72, 190–
91, 193, 201, 211

Statius, 154
Strabo, 199
Sulzer, J. G., 50

T

Taylor, Thomas, 14, 75, 123, 124,
179, 204
Themis, 77
Thetis, 86–88, 90–92
Thomson, James, 60
Tibullus, 73
Tithonus, 65–66
Tooke, John Horn, 49
Torch, 73–76
Trapp, Joseph, 119
Turner, Paul, 139
Typhon, 158–60, 162, 166, 167

V

Venus, 69–73, 75, 167, 180, 202–
3, 205
Virgil: *Aeneid,* 9, 119–22, 123,
134–36, 138, 139, 156–57, 159,
173; *Eclogues,* 118–19, 122–
23, 134, 135; *Georgics,* 119,
124–25

W

Warner, Richard, 66
Will-o'-the-wisp, 126–27, 130
Wilson, Milton, 37–38, 198
Wordsworth, 6

X

Xenophon, 206

Z

Zeno (the Stoic), 80–81